Warrior • 12

German Stormtrooper
1914–18

Ian Drury • Illustrated by Gerry Embleton

First published in Great Britain in 1995 by
Osprey Publishing, Midland House, West Way, Botley,
Oxford OX2 0PH, UK
443 Park Avenue South, New York, NY 10016, USA
Email: info@ospreypublishing.com

CIP Data for this publication is available from
the British Library

ISBN 978 1 85532 372 8

Filmset in Great Britain
Printed in China through World Print Ltd.

07 08 09 10 11 19 18 17 16 15 14 13 12 11 10

FOR A CATALOGUE OF ALL BOOKS PUBLISHED
BY OSPREY PLEASE CONTACT:

NORTH AMERICA
Osprey Direct, C/o Random House Distribution
Center, 400 Hahn Road, Westminster, MD 21157, USA
E-mail: info@ospreydirect.com

ALL OTHER REGIONS
Osprey Direct UK, P.O. Box 140,
Wellingborough, Northants, NN8 2FA, UK
E-mail: info@ospreydirect.co.uk

www.ospreypublishing.com

Author's dedication
For Sue, James and Sophie.

Acknowledgements
This book could not have been completed without the
assistance of David Isby, who tracked down so many
useful sources; Herbert Woodend and Paul Ellis at the
MoD Pattern Room; Richard Brooks; and the members
of Wargames Developments, who have helped clarify
my thoughts about the Western Front.

Artist's note
Readers may care to note that the original paintings
from which the colour plates in this book were prepared are available for private sale. All reproduction
copyright whatsoever is retained by the Publishers. All
enquiries should be addressed to:

www.gerryembleton.com

The Publishers regret that they can enter into no
correspondence upon this matter.

GERMAN STORMTROOPERS

HISTORICAL BACKGROUND

At 6.20 a.m. on 20 November 1917 a thousand guns opened fire on the German trenches defending the town of Cambrai. Under cover of this ferocious bombardment, 376 tanks lumbered across No-Man's Land, spearheading a surprise attack that smashed through the German lines. After three years of trench warfare, the British Army had at last developed the means to crack open the Western Front. The 'green fields beyond' were finally in sight.

For the first time in the war, church bells were rung in England to celebrate a major victory. However, ten days later the Germans counter-attacked. They swiftly recaptured part of the newly created salient, and in some places penetrated beyond the original British frontline. Yet the Germans had no tanks. Their attack was led by units of elite infantry: *Stosstruppen* or 'stormtroops'. Fighting in small groups, amply equipped with light machine guns, mortars, grenade-launchers and hand grenades, they advanced at an equally astonishing rate. By midday on 30 November the leading stormtroops had gained five miles.

Units of *Stosstruppen* had fought in France before, but never in such numbers. Many more would have been available for the counter-stroke at Cambrai, but most stormtroop formations were still in Italy, where they had played a key role in the battle of Caporetto, nearly knocking Italy out of the war, and compelling Britain and France to send sorely needed divisions to shore-up the Italian front. However, the victory at Cambrai counted for more to the German military leadership. It proved that the German army had the capability to rupture the Western Front, to penetrate the defences not only of the gravely weakened Italians, but also of the British Army itself. And unless Germany could achieve victory in the west by the following summer, it was doomed to certain defeat, since the United States' entry into the war had given the Allies overwhelming industrial and numerical superiority.

On 3 December 1917 the Bolshevik leaders were compelled to accept an armistice, taking Russia out of the war. German infantry divisions were already

The earliest shock troops employed by the Germans in 1915. They still wear the distinctive Picklehauber and are laden with grenades, wirecutters and bridging equipment. (G. Embleton)

piling into trains to begin the long journey home, and by the spring of 1918 the German forces on the Western Front had gained 400,000 fresh troops – the last reinforcements they would ever receive.

The German soldiers returning from the east had fought a very different war from their comrades in the west, and they had a great deal to learn before they could participate in the great offensive of 1918. The German infantry on the Western Front had been transformed: gone were the uniformly armed and equipped rifle companies of 1914. The 19th-century style skirmish lines employed that fateful autumn had become a distant memory. Infantry companies no longer fought as monolithic blocs, but divided into platoons that were themselves split into sub-units, each with a discrete tactical role. By late 1916 the organisation of German infantry battalions on the Western Front had begun to foreshadow that of World War II.

In their search for tactical progress on the Western Front, the *Stosstruppen* effectively invented modern infantry tactics. Those employed at Cambrai and throughout 1918 involved individual squads of soldiers using a combination of weapons. The magazine-loading rifle – the sole weapon of the infantry in 1914 – had become just one element in an array of mutually complimentary weapons. While British and French tactics had advanced too, they had not travelled as far or as fast: by 1918 the German stormtroop battalions were using the same sort of 'gun group' and 'rifle group' minor tactics that 2nd Para used at Goose Green in 1982: Indeed, the infantry battle on the desolate ridgeline above Darwin would probably have seemed remarkably familiar to a World War I stormtrooper (although the lack of artillery would have astonished him). Trenches were suppressed by machine gun fire, then assaulted with grenades (in 1918 the stormtroops used cut-down Russian field guns and rifle grenades); particularly difficult bunkers were tackled with heavy weapons.

Like the Parachute Regiment, the stormtroopers had a strong *esprit de corps*. Fit and aggressive shock

troops, they earned their distinctions – and extra rations – by proven bravery on the battlefield. Their training emphasised individual initiative. Non-commissioned officers were no longer there just to enforce the officers' authority, but to provide tactical leadership throughout the platoon.

How the Germans came to develop their battle-winning infantry tactics was a mystery to the Allies. The British learned through bitter experience how successful the Germans' defensive tactics had become, and in 1918 they began to reorganise along the same lines. But stormtroops and their methods were never fully understood. The effects of their actions were painfully clear, but even when it came to writing the official history, the best explanation the British could offer was that the Germans had copied the idea from a French pamphlet.[1]

This book is a concise guide to German stormtroopers in the World War I. In the forefront of tactical development throughout the conflict, they were still associated with victory even after Germany plunged to defeat. In the chaos that followed that defeat, many paramilitary groups modelled themselves in the stormtroops' image. One even hijacked

Kaiser Wilhelm II and General von Moltke at the annual manoeuvres. Despite their almost caricature appearance, the German military leadership gave their subordinates great freedom of action, a policy that encouraged the development of new tactical methods. (US National Archives)

the name. When the then-obscure German Workers' Party organised a gang of toughs to deal with its opponents on the street, it called them the *Sturmabteillung (SA)* ('assault detachment') in conscious imitation. The SA was to become the strong arm of the Nazi party until Adolf Hitler achieved supreme power.

CREATING AN ELITE

The first official German stormtroop unit was authorised on 2 March 1915. OHL[2] ordered the VIII Corps to form a detachment for the testing of experimental weapons and the development of appropriate tactics that could break the deadlock on the Western Front. It was considered a natural job for the Pioneers – the only element of the pre-war army experienced with hand grenades and trained for siege warfare.

For several decades the German Army had been preparing to invade its neighbours. Not entirely

In 1914 most German regiments fought in successive lines of skirmishers with no more than a metre between each man. Because training was decentralised, some units employed looser formations than others. (Private collection)

ignorant of German intentions, the French, Belgian and Russian governments had fortified their frontiers, guarding vital road and rail junctions with modern castles of concrete and steel. While the German Army had acquired the heavy artillery and specialist engineer units to storm such strongpoints, it had not anticipated the stalemate that was to follow its failure to defeat the French Army in 1914.

Machine guns were at the heart of the problem. Even more effective than pre-war studies had suggested, they showed a remarkable ability to survive artillery bombardment in sufficient numbers to mow down attacking infantry. All armies had experienced this, but the armaments company Krupp, in Germany, was first to offer a technical solution. If heavy artillery could not succeed, why not try the opposite tack? Krupp designed the *Sturmkannone* – a 3.7 cm light cannon that could be easily manoeuvred in the frontline – and to test it the first *Sturmabteilung* was created. Commanded by a Pioneer officer, Major

Kaslow of the 18th Pioneer battalion, the detachment became known as *Sturmabteillung Kaslow*. Other equipment they evaluated included steel helmets and body armour. After three months' training the unit was sent into action, parcelled out in detachments to various frontline battalions. The Krupp guns proved cumbersome and vulnerable, and the unit suffered over 30 per cent losses in a series of minor attacks.

Kaslow was replaced in August 1915 by Captain Willy Ernst Rohr, a 37-year-old career soldier from the prestigious *Garde-Schützen* (Guard Rifles) battalion. Under his dynamic leadership, the assault detachment evolved new tactics to break into an enemy trench system. The *Sturmkannone* were replaced by cut-down field guns captured from the Russians, and the soldiers adapted their uniforms and personal equipment to suit their new methods. Combat operations in the Vosges that autumn suggested Rohr's ideas were sound and, in early February 1916 *Sturmabteillung Rohr* was transferred to Verdun. It was expanded to battalion strength on 1 April, and in May OHL ordered all armies on the Western Front to send two officers and four NCOs to Rohr's command to learn the new techniques. *Sturmbataillon Rohr* was to be an instructional unit with a high turnover in personnel, not an elite formation that simply creamed off the most capable soldiers from line regiments.

Formation of *Stosstruppen*

On 23 October 1916 General Ludendorff ordered all German armies in the west to form a battalion of stormtroops. Impressed by an honour guard from *Sturmbataillon Rohr* he had inspected at the Crown Prince's headquarters, Ludendorff soon became aware that the German armies in France and Belgium had changed considerably in the two years he had been away in Russia. By the beginning of December 1916 the 1st, 2nd and 5th German armies each had an assault battalion, and the other 14 German armies established one during the course of the month. However, many of these new *Sturmbataillon* were created by amalgamating existing stormtroop units that had sprung up among the divisions. While Rohr's battalion was created by the high command (and soon won powerful friends, including the Crown Prince, von Falkenhayn and ultimately Ludendorff), it had no monopoly of new tactical ideas. Since mid-1915 some German regiments had been creating small units of shock troops from within their own ranks. These select troops operated in sections, platoons and even whole companies, and enjoyed a variety of titles. Many favoured *Sturmtrupp* (assault troop), but others included *Jagdkommando* (hunting commando) and *Patrouillentrupp* (raid troop). When the first flamethrower units were assembled in early 1915, under Captain Reddemann, he called his men *Stosstruppen* (stormtroops). This caught the soldiers' imagination and, regardless of their unit's actual title, the men of these first assault detachments began to refer to themselves as *Stosstruppen*.

OHL did not intend the stormtroops to be a permanent feature of the German order of battle but

Communications were the greatest problem on the battlefields of World War I: this recently entrenched German command post could expect to have most of its telephone lines cut by the first enemy bombardment. As the war progressed, the Germans granted greater freedom to local commanders, relying on their individual initiative in the absence of reliable communications. (US Army Signal Corps)

a model for the rest of the army. Once this had been achieved, the stormtroop formations were to disappear. Consequently, the stormtroop battalions were never incorporated into the peacetime army structure and were never assigned home barracks or recruiting areas in Germany. They were not associated with historical regiments from the 18th century in the way regular regiments embraced their military heritage; nor did they receive colours.

By November 1916 more than 30 German divisions included some sort of assault detachment. Several independent corps, *Landwehr* divisions and even the Naval division had also established a stormtrooper unit on their own initiative. This remarkable process of parallel development stemmed from the training methods and doctrine of the pre-war German Army. In all other major armies training methods were determined by the high command, but the 22 corps districts of the Imperial German Army were fiercely independent. While the renowned General Staff planned German strategy, peacetime troop movements were left entirely to the corps commanders, who reported directly to the Kaiser. This tradition of tactical independence paid handsome dividends after 1914. The general staffs of other armies worked equally hard to solve the tactical problems of the Western Front, but many handicapped themselves by trying to micro-manage the frontline battle. German regimental officers, accustomed to less interference in their tactics, had more freedom to experiment. As a result, by the summer of 1915 stormtroop units were springing up throughout the German armies in the west. *Sturmbataillon Rohr* would be the most famous, and was instrumental in winning official approval for stormtroops, but the simultaneous appearance of assault detachments in so many divisions demonstrates just how successfully the German military system encouraged individual initiative.

UNIFORMS

German infantrymen began World War I in one of the more practical uniforms worn by the rival armies. Although the style of the German field service dress harked back to the glory days of 1870, the 1910-pattern *feldgrau* uniform was eminently suitable for the opening campaigns of 1914. However, once the German Army went on the defensive in the west, the soldiers' appearance began to change. One of the first casualties was the *Pickelhaube* itself. Its spike served no practical purpose but was the first part of a German soldier to become visible if he peered over the parapet, and frontline soldiers soon dispensed with it. The M1915 *Pickelhaube* featured a detachable spike, and the drab cloth cover worn over it lost the red regimental number on the front. The con-

struction of the M1915-pattern *Picklehaube* reveals a second influence on the German soldiers' appearance, and one that would prove almost as significant as the demands of trench warfare: the effect of the Allied blockade. The *Picklehaube* was supposed to be made from boiled leather, but felt, thin metal and even compressed cardboard were tried as substitutes.

The stormtroop detachments in 1915 wore standard service uniforms. During that year, the appearance of the frontline troops differed only in minor detail from that of 1914. In a change agreed before the war, *Steingrau* (stone grey) trousers were introduced to replace the *Feldgrau* ones because the latter seem to have faded too quickly. The M1907–10 tunic was superseded by a more utilitarian version – the distinctive cuffs were replaced by plain turnbacks, and the false skirt pocket flaps disappeared. Soldiers were supposed to blacken their leather equipment, including their boots, belts and cartridge pouches, but this was not always possible in the frontline, as captured equipment shows.

Wartime Equipment

From 1915 soldiers were issued with a new piece of defensive equipment – one that was to prove indispensable when the German scientists introduced their so-called 'higher form of killing'. The M1915 respirator had a rubberised fabric face piece and a detachable filter (soldiers carried a spare). The increase in the use of poison gas by both sides compelled soldiers to carry respirators and to rig up gas alarms in their frontline positions. It also added a unique element of horror to the battlefield. However, for all the suffering it caused, this ghastly application of industrial technology failed to break the deadlock.

On 21 September 1915 the German army introduced a completely new infantry uniform. The *Bluse* (blouse) was supposed to replace both earlier tunics, although the 1907/10 and 1914 patterns remained in use until the end of the war. Cut slightly looser, it has two large slanted pockets at the front, and looks rather more like a modern combat jacket than the 19th-century style of the earlier tunics. The front buttons – metal, painted grey – are concealed behind

Sturmbataillon Rohr tested several types of body armour in 1915, rejecting all but the steel helmet as too cumbersome to fight in. This elaborate breastplate was subsequently issued to some snipers and sentries. (IWM)

Stormtroopers are inspected outside their rest billets before going into the line. Note the sandbags bulging with stick grenades, and the puttees and boots that have replaced the pre-war jackboots. (IWM)

a flap, and the shoulder straps are detachable. Manufactured in a dark field grey, it has a fall-down collar faced with green. As before, the jackets of *Jäger* and *Schützen* regiments were dyed a much greener shade of *Feldgrau*.

The M1895 knapsack, with its distinctive cow hide back, was too cumbersome for trench warfare. While it remained on issue until 1918 and was worn in action on the Russian Front, by late 1915 German infantry in France and Belgium had began to use an 'assault pack'. They wrapped their greatcoat in a tent cloth and rolled it around a mess tin, creating a smaller, handier pack, more suited to their needs. Their old knapsacks would be used when marching behind the lines, but were often put into battalion stores while the infantry were in the frontline.

The first article of uniform that distinguished a stormtrooper from a regular infantryman appeared in early 1916. In time, it would become the trademark of the German soldier in both World Wars. Its very shape has such an emotional charge that the US Army agonised throughout the 1970s before introducing its similarly shaped kevlar helmet – soon dubbed the 'Fritz'. The M1916 *Stahlhelm* was part of a range of body armour tested by the German Army from 1915. Dubbed by the British the 'coal scuttle' helmet, it was made from silicon-nickel steel and

weighed 1.2 kg. Extending over the ears and back of the neck, it offered better protection than either the French M1915 mild-steel 'Adrian' helmet or the revived medieval design favoured by the British. It was padded inside and adjusted by leather straps to fit each individual. Thick lugs projected from either side to support an additional steel plate across the front of the helmet. The *Stahlhelm* was issued to sentries and snipers, but was rarely seen by ordinary riflemen.

From its inception, *Sturmabteilung Rohr* was used to test body armour that might be effective in No-Man's Land. The early stormtroops experimented with shields rather like those used today for riot control; but in those pre-Kevlar days, the German shields were made from solid steel and proved too heavy to use during an attack. The protection they offered could not compensate for the loss of mobility. Steel breastplates were similarly restrictive, and tended to be worn by look-outs or other exposed personnel in static positions.

The German Army's pre-war interest in siege warfare paid an unexpected bonus in the autumn of

1914: the arsenals of its border fortresses were packed with hand grenades, originally intended for use by the garrisons. These were shipped to the frontline, where they gave the Germans a useful advantage during the first months of trench warfare. Since only the Pioneers had been trained in their use, individual Pioneers were posted to infantry battalions as supervisors. During 1915 two new types of grenade entered production and soon became standard weapons: the *Eierhandgranate (*egg grenade) and the *Stielhandgranate (*stick grenade).

By February 1916, when the German Army launched its great offensive at Verdun, stormtroop detachments had begun to assume a rather different appearance from soldiers in regular infantry battalions. Stormtroops were among the first to receive the new steel helmet; most of the 5th German Army's infantry were still wearing the *Picklehaube* with the spike removed. The stormtroops spearheading the attack were well equipped with stick grenades, each carrying a dozen or more in a sandbag slung across their chest. Captain Rohr's men had also substituted ankle boots and puttees for their 1866-pattern leather jackboots – another practice that was to spread throughout the assault units over the following two years. The stormtroopers had also started sewing leather patches on their elbows and knees – shielding their most vulnerable joints from the wear and tear of

The Crown Prince inspects a newly formed battalion of stormtroops before the Great Offensive of 1918. Note some officers still wearing the out-dated Picklehaube, *and the ammunition pouches being worn by the soliders on the right of the picture. (IWM)*

crawling. The first wave over the top at Verdun was primarily armed with hand grenades, so the men carried their rifles slung and did not wear the issue belt and shoulder harness that supported the ammunition pouches. Extra clips of 7.92 mm cartridges were carried in cloth bandoliers, each holding 70 rounds.

By the end of 1916 official stormtroop battalions were established throughout the western armies. Soldiers were selected from regular battalions, posted to a stormtroop formation for a period and then returned to their original unit. A typical infantry battalion of mid-1917 would have included a number of officers and junior NCOs who had served in a stormtroop formation. Exact figures are impossible to obtain, since a high proportion of the Imperial Army's records was destroyed by RAF Bomber Command in 1945.

Men who had served with the stormtroops may well have returned with different uniforms as well as different tactical ideas. In his autobiographical novel, *Krieg*, Ludwig Renn has a newly arrived officer say to an NCO: '*You are wearing puttees and leather knee-*

pieces. Is that allowed in the regiment, sergeant-major?' Learning that the man has just returned from a storm battalion, the captain is delighted, and plans a whole platoon of assault troops. But Renn implies that some line officers were not best pleased with NCOs returning to the battalion with personalised uniforms – and a new sense of their own importance. Renn's real name was Arnold von Golssenau, and he was a career officer who may have encountered such an attitude among his colleagues.

WEAPONS

Rifles and Carbines

In 1914 German infantry regiments were uniformly armed with the 1898-pattern Mauser rifle. Chambered for the 8×57 mm rimless cartridge, it held five rounds in an internal box magazine that was loaded through the action by brass stripper clips. The side of the stock was cut away on the right, allowing the soldier to slide the cartridges in with the flat of his thumb, rather than push them down with the tip. This has a practical advantage over the British Lee-Enfield (SMLE) in which you had to press home the rounds with the end of your thumb, sometimes splintering the nail in your haste to get the rifle back into action. On the other hand, because it is cocked on opening, the Mauser bolt is less tolerant of poor quality ammunition and dirt around the breach. You cannot retain your sight picture while working the Mauser's action, and the magazine only holds half as many rounds as an SMLE. The Germans attempted to increase the Mauser's firepower by issuing a 25-round magazine, but it only appeared in limited numbers and was rather awkward to handle. With its backsight down, the M1898 was sighted to 200 metres, and it could be elevated by 50-metre increments to a maximum of 2,000 metres. Weighing 4 kg unloaded, and 1,250 mm long, the M1898 was a robust and accurate weapon, ideally suited to the open warfare of 1914, but not for the trench fighting that followed.

The German Army issued carbines to all other arms: cavalry, artillery, pioneers, independent machine gun companies and motor transport units. The only infantry units to use them at the beginning of the war were the *Jäger* and *Schützen* battalions. The standard carbine was the M1898AZ (*Karabiner 98*

A stormtroop company poses for a group photograph during 1918. It is at less than half its established strength in riflemen, but it includes two MG '08s and one MG '08/15. (IWM)

mit Aufplanz- und Zusammensetzvorrichtung), which was 1,090 mm long and had a 590 mm barrel instead of the 600 mm of the M1898. Two much shorter carbines had been tested before the war, but were rejected because the muzzle-flash and recoil from a 435 mm barrel proved unacceptable.

Sturmbataillon Rohr adopted the K.98 carbine during 1915, and it slowly became the standard armament of stormtroop formations throughout the German armies in the west. It was significantly shorter, and thus handier in the confines of the trenches; but at prevailing combat ranges, it was no less accurate or hard-hitting. When it came to re-arm in the 1930s, the German Army adopted a new Mauser with similar dimensions to the K.98 for all infantry units.

Automatic Weapons

The stormtroop battalions also received the world's first effective sub-machine gun, the MP18. Designed by Hugo Schmiesser, the MP18 introduced most of the features that were to make the sub-machine gun the key close-quarter weapon of World War II.

Chambered for 9 mm Parabellum, the MP18 fired from the open bolt: pulling the trigger, sent the bolt forward, where it stripped the uppermost round from the magazine, chambered it and fired it. If the trigger was held back, the bolt continued to cycle driven directly back by the propellant gas and flung forward again by the return spring. It was mechanically simple, and highly effective. Over 30,000 were supplied to the German Army during 1918, but most of them arrived after the great March offensive. General Ludendorff looked to the MP18 to increase the defensive power of the German infantry as the Allies began their assault on the Hindenburg Line.

Some soldiers in the stormtroop battalions had had experience with rapid-fire weapons, if not automatics. NCOs in charge of machine gun or mortar teams were often equipped with pistols capable of doubling as a carbine. Both the P.'08 Luger and the 'Broomhandle' Mauser were capable of receiving a shoulder stock which gave them an effective range of over 100 yards. More practically, it gave the NCOs a handy self-defence weapon that was much better than a rifle when enemy bombing parties were closing in. For close-quarter fighting in the enemy trenches, an Artillery Model Luger with a 32-round 'snail' magazine made much more sense than a bolt-action rifle with a five-round magazine. As Erwin Rommel observed: '*In a man-to-man fight, the winner is he who has one more round in his magazine.*'[3]

Hand Grenades

The Pioneers' hand grenades of 1914 were soon replaced by far more effective weapons. The M1915 *Stielhandgranate* is the most famous, and it became almost the primary weapon of the assault battalions. When stormtroop detachments led the attack at Verdun in February 1916, many of them went into action with their rifles slung, leaving their hands free to lob stick grenades into surviving French positions. The stick grenade consisted of a hollow cylinder about 100 mm long and 75 mm in diameter containing an explosive mixture of potassium perchlorate, barium nitrate, black powder and powdered aluminium. The cylinder had a metal clip on the side.

The light flamethrower was operated by two men: one carried the tank of fuel and compressed nitrogen, the other aimed the hose.

Early models had to be lit manually, which proved dangerous; later versions incorporated an automatic ignition system. (IWM)

The standard German infantry rifle was the Gewehr 98 (top), but other troops were issued with the Karabiner 98a (middle). This was soon adopted by the stormtroopers, and some G.98s were converted to carbines during the war (bottom). Note that the K.98 is fully stocked and has a turn-down bolt, less likely to snag on a stormtrooper's kit. (Pattern Room Collection)

enabling it to be attached to a belt. It also had a hollow wooden throwing handle 225 mm long. A cord projected from the bulbous end; pulling it ignited a friction tube that detonated the main charge 5½ seconds later. Some were issued with 7-second fuses, others with 3-second fuses; the type of fuse was stamped on the handle. There was also a percussion-fused version, detonated by a spring-powered striker when it hit the ground.

In 1916 German infantry began to receive a new grenade, the *Eierhandgranate* or 'egg grenade'. Weighing 310 grammes (11 oz) it was made of cast iron, painted black and was the size and shape of a hen's egg. A friction lighter ignited a 5-second fuse, although an 8-second fuse was available if it was fired from a grenade launcher. This tiny grenade could be thrown as far as 50 metres by an experienced grenadier, but its explosive effect was fairly limited. The egg grenade was first encountered by the British on the Somme: stormtroops counter-attacked north of Thiepval in July 1916, hurling the new grenades into captured trenches and re-taking most of the original German frontline.

Both main types of German grenade relied primarily on blast rather than fragmentation, and they were far more effective in the confines of a trench than in the open field. Stormtroopers assaulting particularly well-defended positions tended to tape batches of stick grenades together and then post these deadly packages over the enemy parapet or into the slits of concrete bunkers.

Machine Guns

The German Army did not take to machine guns with the same readiness as the British and French armies: only in 1913 were they issued to line infantry regiments. However, wartime experience soon vindicated the machine gun lobby of the pre-war army, and the number of machine gun companies rose rapidly. In 1914 each infantry regiment included a six-gun machine gun company. During 1915 regiments received supplementary machine gun sections of 30–40 men and three or four machine guns, and by the end of the year many regiments had two full-strength machine gun companies. In the winter of 1915/16 specialist machine gun units, known as machine gun marksmen (*Maschinengewehr Scharf-schützen Trupps*) were created. Trained specifically for offensive use of machine guns, their personnel underwent a four- or five-week instruction course and were formed into independent companies of six guns. They were first seen at the frontline at Verdun.

By mid-1916 the ad hoc development of machine gun units had left some regiments with as many as 25 machine guns, and others with their regulation six. In August a new standard organisation was adopted: all machine gun companies were to consist of six weapons and all infantry regiments were to have three such companies, one attached to each infantry

The MP18 was one of the first sub-machine guns to be used in action. Note the 32-round 'snail' magazine, developed for the Artillery Model Luger, and its loading tool. The magazine affects the balance of the MP18, canting the weapon sharply to the left even when empty. (Pattern Room Collection)

battalion. The machine gun marksmen companies were grouped into machine gun detachments (*Maschinen-Gewehr Scharfschützen-Abteilungen*) each of three companies. One such detachment was normally attached to each division engaged in active operations at the front. When the divisional *Sturmbataillone* were formed in December 1916, each battalion had either one or two machine gun companies.

The number of German machine gun units continued to increase during 1917, although the number of machine gun companies per regiment remained the same. Machine gun companies were expanded to eight, ten and finally 12 weapons per company, and the number of independent companies was increased too. A stormtroop battalion could have anything from 12 to 24 machine guns, while independent *Sturmkompagnien* had their own machine gun platoon of two weapons.

Machine gun companies were equipped with the *Maschinen-Gewehr* '08, a modified Maxim gun design. The gun itself weighed 25 kg (55 lb); on its stout metal sledge and with its water-jacket filled, it weighed 63.6 kg (140 lb) and was not the most mobile of infantry weapons. Although the MG '08 was to exact a fearful toll of Allied infantrymen, it was primarily a defensive weapon. It did not break down to manageable loads and it was a struggle to move it across the heavily cratered battlefields of the Western Front. Nevertheless, when the German 5th army made its supreme effort at Verdun, in June 1916, attacking regiments put their machine gun companies in the front line. The Bavarian Life Guard,

supported by *Sturmbataillon Rohr* seized the village of Fleury and brought up 24 MG '08s to fight its way through the ruins.

Light Machine Guns

The German Army recognised the need for a lighter machine gun in 1915, and work began on a modification of the MG '08 design. In the meantime, since most of Germany's enemies were already using light machine guns, the German army formed special battalions to use captured enemy weapons. The first *Musketen-Bataillone* were created in August 1915 and committed to the Champagne battle in September. These units were armed with Madsen light machine guns, captured from the Russians. The Danish-designed Madsen was a true light machine gun: air-cooled, bipod-mounted and weighing just under 10 kg, it was fed by a 20-round box magazine. The Russian Army had bought the Madsen for its cavalry before the war and it took little effort to re-chamber the weapons. Each *Musketen-Bataillon* consisted of three companies, each with four officers, 160 of other ranks and 30 machine guns. A four-man squad operated each weapon, and the soldiers also carried K.98s, like the regimental machine gun companies.

The *Mustketen-Bataillone* were used during the battle of the Somme as part of the German second line. When a breakthrough occurred, they were rushed to plug the gap, machine-gunning the leading Allied units and inviting the inevitable attention of British artillery. They suffered heavy casualties, and lost all their Madsens by the end of the campaign.

The British Army was already using the Lewis gun: a heavier weapon, weighing closer to 15 kg, but far easier to manoeuvre than an MG '08. With a 47-round drum magazine, it could not deliver the sort of sustained fire of a belt-fed weapon, but it gave an infantry platoon the means to suppress an enemy position without relying on heavy weapons further back. By the end of the Somme battle, enough Lewis guns had fallen into German hands for the *Musketen* battalions to re-equip with them. Also re-chambered for German ammunition, the Lewis guns remained in use until the *Musketen* battalions were converted to *Maschinen-Gewehr Scharfschützen* battalions, in April 1918. By then, all German infantry regiments contained so many light machine guns, there was no purpose in having a handful of battalions armed exclusively with them. However, the stormtroop battalions seem to have liked the Lewis gun so much that many retained them in preference to the later light machine guns produced by the Germans. Lewis guns remained in frontline service until the end of the war, with captured weapons repaired and converted in a factory in Brussels.

Loading a 24.5 cm heavy Minenwerfer (old model) had to be done carefully: they were prone to burst owing to premature detonation of the shell. Extreme cold increased the danger by making the barrels brittle. (US Army Signal Corps)

In December 1916 the German Army introduced its 'official' light machine gun, the Model '08/15 – basically an MG '08 mounted on a bipod and fitted with a wooden rifle butt and pistol grip. It was still water-cooled, but the casing was narrower. Weighing 19.5 kg (43 lb) it was only 'light' in the imagination of its designers. On the other hand, it was arguably the world's first general purpose machine gun (GPMG): light enough to be manhandled over the battlefield, but heavy enough to deliver sustained fire. Fed by 100- or 250-round belts, the MG '08/15 could provide a much greater volume of fire than the Lewis or Chauchat light machine guns being used by the Allies and, despite its weight, it anticipated the tactical role of the MG34 in World War II.

The MG '08/15 was first encountered on the Western Front in the spring of 1917, when German infantry companies each received three. This increased to six over the course of the year, although units on the Eastern Front were a lower priority, and most made do with a pair of MG '08/15s until the Russian campaign was over. The MG '08/15s were initially organised as discrete units, effectively forming a fourth platoon in each rifle company rather as the British infantry platoons added a Lewis section to their three infantry sections. As the numbers of MG '08/15s increased, they were integrated into the platoons, giving platoon commanders the ability to manoeuvre their rifle sections covered by the suppressive fire of the machine guns.

Grenade-launchers

The German Army began the war with two types of rifle grenade in service. Both weighed just under a kilo and were fired from the *Gewehr* 98 rifle, using a special blank cartridge. Recoil was vicious and accuracy minimal, but once the trenchlines were established, troops rigged up all manner of improvised mountings. By 1916 a purpose-built *Granatenwerfer* (Grenade-thrower) had been introduced. It weighed 40 kg, but broke down into two loads – the thrower (23 kg) and the platform (15 kg). It had a maximum range of 350 m and a minimum range of 50 m. Infantry regiments had 12 each by 1916, and with them special 'rebounding' grenades were introduced. The latter carried a separate black powder charge so that when the grenade struck the ground, it was blown back into the air a fraction of a second before it

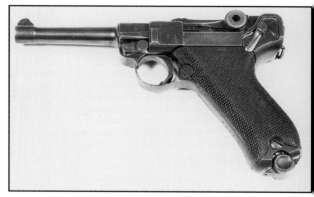

The German Army's standard service pistol was the Pistole '08 *, better known by the name of its inventor, the* Luger. *With an 8-round magazine and one in the breech, the* Luger *had a clear edge over the six-shot revolvers favoured by the Allies. Note the serial number '1'; this is the first* Luger *manufactured by Erfurt in 1916. (Pattern Room Collection)*

detonated. The *Granatenwerfer* could also launch signal rockets. This handy two-man weapon could deliver an impressive hail of fire against enemy strongpoints; its ammunition was light, and if enough infantrymen carried forward sandbags full of grenades, the *Granatenwerfer* could support them with both direct and indirect fire.

Mortars

After witnessing the success of Japanese improvised mortars at Port Arthur, the German Army ordered a series of purpose-built weapons for the Pioneers. By

1914 the Pioneers had three types of *Minenwerfer* at their disposal: the 7.6 cm light mortar that threw a 4.7 kg bomb out to 1,050 m; the medium 17 cm mortar that fired a 49.5 kg bomb 900 m; and the heavy 21 cm mortar that delivered a 100 kg bomb up to 550 m. The latter was originally intended for the defence of fortresses, and was the deadliest weapon on the Western Front. Its very high trajectory and heavy charges could bring about the collapse of whole sections of trench. The mortars' noise, and slow, remorseless passage through the air added to the terror. New versions of all three mortars were introduced in 1916; these had much longer ranges and were capable of delivering gas-filled projectiles.

The trench mortars were assigned to the siege train in 1914, but although they remained nominally in the hands of Pioneers, they were soon reorganised into independent mortar detachments. Their personnel were largely drawn from the infantry, and they were attached to the infantry on a basis of one *Minnenwerfer Abteillung* per regiment. Each regimental detachment consisted of 12 7.6 cm mortars and 24 grenade-launchers. The heavier mortars were grouped into *Minenwerfer* companies, with one normally attached to each division. Each company comprised three sections: one heavy (four 24 cm or 25 cm mortars) and two medium (eight 17 cm mortars). There were also at least 13 *Minenwerfer* battalions as a reserve at the disposal of General Headquarters, that could be sent to support German attacks or to

reinforce a hard-pressed sector. A *Minenwerfer* battalion had four companies, each equipped with six heavy and four light mortars.

Stormtroop battalions usually included a mortar company of their own. Independent *Sturmkompagnien* generally had a section of up to four light mortars.

Flamethrowers

Soldiers from the Pioneer units were already incorporated into the stormtroop detachments. On 18 January 1915 an all-volunteer formation of Pioneers was created to operate the newly developed flamethrowers. By a curious twist of fate, the commander of the *Flammenwerfer Abteillung*, Major Herman Reddeman, was a former chief of the Leipzig fire brigade. He had been conducting experiments with flame weapons for several years before the war, and had collaborated with Richard Fiedler, the man credited with perfecting the first operational flamethrower. Two types were tested in combat: a man-pack version (*Kleines Flammenwerfer*) operated by two men, and a static version (*Grosses Flammenwerfer*) that projected a jet of flame for 40 m. To operate the former, one man carried the fuel tank on his back, while a second man aimed the tube. Compressed nitrogen expelled fuel oil which was ignited as it left the nozzle. It was tested in February 1915 against the French near Verdun, and in June against the British. In both cases the terror inspired

Left: Stormtroop battalions included a battery of artillery – usually these cut-down Russian 76.2 cm field guns, with an effective range of 1,000 metres. Used to engage enemy machine gun positions, they were hand pulled since horses were too vulnerable. (IWM)

Right: German artillery, machine gun and Minenwerfer crews carried rifles and pistols for self-defence. The Artillery Model Luger and Mauser C96 were particularly favoured because they doubled as light carbines, accurate at up to 100 metres when fitted with a shoulder-stock. (Pattern Room Collection)

by jets of liquid flame enabled the German assault troops to capture their objectives with relative ease. No man was prepared to remain in a trench with blazing fuel oil cascading over the parapet.

The *Flammenwerfer Abteillung* became the 3rd Guard Pioneer battalion. Initially composed of six companies, by 1917 it had expanded to 12 companies, a workshop detachment and a regimental headquarters. Each flamethrower company consisted of 20 large and 18 small flamethrowers. A platoon (*Flammenwerfertrupp*) of between four and eight small flamethrowers was attached to most stormtroop battalions.

Artillery

The Krupp 3.7 cm cannon tested in 1915 had proved a disappointment, but the Germans remained convinced that the best counter to an enemy machine gun nest was a small field gun that used direct fire. The *Sturmkannone* was duly replaced by a mountain howitzer that could be manhandled across the battlefield. However, in early 1916 the stormtroopers received a specially converted field gun, the 7.62 cm *Infanterie Geschütz*. This was the standard Russian field-piece with its barrel shortened from 2.28 m to 1.25 m, new sights graduated to 1,800 m, and a low recoil carriage with wheels only 1.1 m in diameter. It fired a 5.9 kg (13 lb) shell of German manufacture. By 1917 there were 50 infantry gun batteries on the Western Front; each stormtroop battalion included one, and the others were brought forward for the close defence of threatened sectors or as support for local offensives. They were also used as anti-tank guns. Batteries consisted of either four or six guns.

During 1917 the Germans supplemented the infantry gun batteries with another 50 or so 'close-range batteries' (*Nahkampf-Batterien*) each of four 7.7 cm field guns on special low-wheeled carriages. Instead of being fixed directly on the axle, the gun was mounted on trunnions forward of it. These batteries had neither transport nor horses, and were used primarily as anti-tank guns firing semi-armour-piercing ammunition.

RECRUITMENT

Every German male was liable for military service from his 17th to his 45th birthday, but parliamentary opposition to the spiralling military budget helped ensure that less than half the young men eligible were actually called to the colours before 1914. Senior officers were also conscious that while the general

A German 'trench gun' in action. Some 50 'close range' batteries were added to the German forces on the Western Front in 1917, serving as anti-tank guns in 1918. Note the size and low profile of the bullet-proof shield. (IWM)

A German machine gun platoon on the march during the second battle of the Somme, 1918. They are equipped with captured

British Lewis guns, which were used extensively by German machine gun units after 1916. (IWM)

population had increased by 50 per cent since 1870, the Prussian nobility had not bred as quickly. Expanding the army too rapidly would necessitate commissioning officers from outside the *Junker* class – an act so unthinkable that it was never fully implemented, even during the war.

In the three years before World War I, only 45 per cent of Germany's potential military manpower went into the army. In 1914 the German Empire could mobilise an army of 4.9 million men from a total population of 67.5 million. France, acutely aware of its numerical inferiority, had trained all its young men but the disabled, and fielded 5 million soldiers from a population of just 39.5 million.

Between the ages of 17 and 20, German men were theoretically liable for service in the *Landsturm*. Service with the regular army began at 20 and consisted of two years' duty with the standing army and three for those posted to the cavalry or horse artillery. After completing regular service, men were assigned to the reserve for four or five years respec-

tively, and were liable to be called up for two weeks' refresher training each September. When a man reached 27, his liability for frontline service was over, and he was transferred to the *Landwehr*. At the age of 39, men were re-assigned to the *Landsturm*, essentially a militia intended only for garrison duties. The high proportion of young men not selected for military service were not forgotten, but were assigned to the *Erstaz-reserve* (supplementary reserve) for 12 years, and were theoretically liable for a little basic training. In 1914 this pool of untrained manpower provided a reserve of a million men in their twenties, and it was used to bring a succession of new reserve units to full strength.

Drain on Manpower

The annual recruit contingent or class (*Jahresklasse*) consisted of all men who reached the age of 20 in a given year. During the war Germany's enemies closely monitored the arrival of each class in the frontline, since the timing of each call-up revealed just how quickly German manpower was being expended.

Germany went to war in 1914 with the same passionate enthusiasm that gripped so many European nations. Thousands of young men volunteered

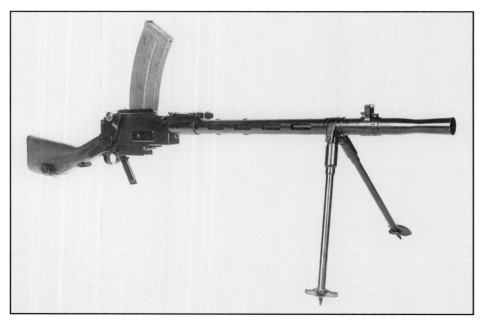

The Germans captured enough Danish-made Madsen light machine guns from the Russians to equip a number of Musketen battalions. These specialist light machine gun units fought on the Western Front during 1916, sustaining heavy losses on the Somme. (Pattern Room Collection)

for service ahead of their conscription class, and the German Army expanded beyond its anticipated strength. The class of 1914 was called up at its normal time – the end of September – but there was a delay of several months before all the recruits were taken into the depots. The men of the *Ersatz-Reserve* were being organised into new reserve divisions.[4] Meanwhile the existing Reserve and *Landwehr* formations took their place in the German order of battle. The *Landsturm* was drawn upon to make up the losses, and was all but exhausted by the end of 1915.

The class of 1915 was called up between April and June 1915 (four months early). Yet this was not enough, and the class of 1916 was called up between August and November – a full year early. Nevertheless, each class received four to five months' training before being posted to the frontline. When the German Army suffered over 300,000 losses during 1915, steps were taken to comb out more personnel, men previously rejected as unfit were re-examined under more stringent criteria, and many found themselves in uniform after all. The class of 1917 was called up from January 1916 (over 18 months early). Training time was reduced to three months as the holocausts of Verdun and the Somme shattered whole divisions. Writing after the war, several senior officers regarded 1916 as critical: the year the last of the peacetime-trained German Army perished.

The class of 1918 was called up from September 1916, and the first of these 18-year-old recruits were at the front by January 1917. Many of these young men were organised into new infantry formations.[5] The class of 1919 was in uniform by the summer of 1917, but most of these teenage recruits were dispatched to the Russian Front to release more experienced soldiers for service in the west.

Most German soldiers ignored regulations and kept diaries, often filled with details about their own unit and those of their friends. But they were given official documents that told the Allies even more; their paybook showed which class they belonged to, and from their company payroll number, the Allies could calculate how many men had been through a particular unit. Each soldier was alloted a number when he joined his unit, and if he was killed, captured or invalided out, his replacement would be given the succeeding number. It was very logical, but very useful for enemy intelligence. The British Army had an officer at GHQ whose sole duty was the analysis of captured paybooks. British records show that, for example, a company of the 202nd Reserve infantry regiment included men from the class of 1918 as early as April 1917. By September, the only members of earlier classes remaining in the regiment were returned sick or wounded.

Recruitment into the assault battalions was voluntary from 1915 until late 1917. Standards in the early *Sturmbataillone* were so high that when four *Jäger* battalions were converted to stormtroops, more than 500 men had to be transferred out as unsuitable. Although officers could be posted to a stormtroop unit compulsorily, men of other ranks were supposed to be under 25 years old, unmarried and with a good sports record. With Ludendorff's endorsement, the training role of the stormtroop battalions expanded. Soldiers, and especially NCOs, spent a limited period with an assault battalion before returning to their original unit.

Re-organisation for 1918 Campaign

The steady depletion of German manpower eventually frustrated Ludendorff's intention of raising all divisions to stormtrooper standard. In the winter of 1917/18, as he planned Germany's do-or-die offensive in the west, Ludendorff realised he faced an insuperable demographic problem: too many men in the ranks were in their thirties, or unable to meet the physical demands of the new tactics. His solution was to reorganise the army, concentrating the young and fit into attack divisions.[6] These received a disproportionately large share of artillery support, ammunitions, rations and training time. Ludendorff assembled them into an elite striking force that, in 1918, would achieve the first major breakthrough on the Western Front. However, for every attack division, there were now three trench divisions (*Stellungsdivisionen*) of marginal fighting value. An uninspiring mixture of the old and very young, they were less well equipped and certainly less motivated. Ludendorff's reorganisation is the origin of the myth that stormtroopers were like the World War II special forces: elite units recruited at the expense of less glamorous line battalions. In fact the organisation of the original stormtrooper battalions had not sucked the lifeblood of 'ordinary' regiments; they had been training units, and their personnel had eventually returned to their original regiments to pass on new ideas and methods and contribute to a constant 'levelling up' of tactical skill.

TRAINING

Ludwig Renn's novel describes the experiences of a sergeant posted to a stormtroop battalion in the winter of 1917: '*We had to drag machine guns, fling bombs, advance along trenches and crawl without a sound. At first it was a severe strain on me. I sweated on every occasion and several times everything reeled around me, but only for a short time. Then, daily it grew easier. We were on duty from morning to night with only two or three hours of an interval at midday. I had no time for reflection and felt in good trim.*'[7]

Skeletal remains of a German soldier lie in an abandoned position. Constant artillery fire made it hard enough to evacuate the wounded, let alone the dead. Bodies buried in the frontline were frequently disinterred by enemy shells. (US National Archives)

British soldiers pull away a captured heavy Minenwerfer. The short range of the pre-war mortars forced the Germans to deploy them in the frontline, where they were vulnerable to capture if the Allies attacked. (Private collection)

Renn's hero was not alone: a high proportion of the German Army was retraining that winter. As outlined above, the Army was being reorganised into 'attack' and 'fortress' divisions; the fittest men were concentrated in the former, and the very best among them were posted to the stormtroop battalions.

The First Units

Captain Rohr's stormtroop detachment had effectively been a training unit since its inception. In December 1915 it hosted a cadre from the 12th *Landwehr* division, instructing several hundred officers and men in the new tactics. The *Landwehr* troops learned how to fight in platoons and sections, rather than lining up each rifle company in a traditional skirmish line. They learned to use 1:5,000 scale maps of enemy positions, rehearsing their attacks on full-scale mock-ups of the French lines. For the first time, NCOs found themselves given a real job of leadership – making their own tactical decisions.

In 1916, after its performance at Verdun had proved the value of stormtrooper tactics, Rohr's battalion established a base at the nearby town of Beauville. It had barely begun a training programme for the four *Jäger* battalions scheduled to become stormtroop units when the Brusilov offensive and Rumanian declaration of war forced OHL to dis-

patch three of the battalions to the Eastern Front. Only the 3rd (Brandenburg) *Jäger* battalion was retrained, becoming the 3rd *Jäger-Sturmbataillon* on 4 August 1916, and 500 men had to be transferred from the battalion as unfit for the physical demands of the new role. The training programme involved repeated live fire exercises over dummy trenches, with flamethrower, trench mortar and infantry gun detachments all in action.

The numerous stormtrooper battalions established in December 1916 were regarded primarily as training units. Selected officers and NCOs from each infantry division served brief tours of duty with an army-level stormtroop battalion, returning to their formation to pass on what they had learned. The stormtroop battalions did not spend their time in the frontline, but remained at bases in the rear, though occasionally they would be brought forward to undertake trench raids or local offensives. Many assault battalions were alloted motor transport – a rarity in the German Army – so their transit to and from the battlefield was as rapid as possible.

The offensive at Caporetto was preceded by a period of specialised training in mountain warfare. Troops assigned to the operation were sent to the 14th army front in September 1917 to acclimatise them; they undertook progressively longer marches in the thin Alpine air in preparation. Further weapons training was also required, as they were issued with three MG '08/15s per company during that month. (The MG '08/15 was nearly as complex as the full-size MG '08, and almost impossible to keep in action without a fully trained crew.) The extra firepower was a blessing, but there was a constant shortage of trained machine gunners for the rest of the war.

Retraining the Infantry

German infantry training altered during the war. The time allocated to recruits' basic training was reduced, but the content of their instruction became more relevant. General Ludendorff was not the

pompous martinet he appeared. He had no time for the niceties of drill: it was irrelevant on the modern battlefield, and he likened it to dog training. (He had a similar regard for the sort of methods used to 'break in' recruits in more recent times.) Endless drill, he remarked, simply deprives young men of their personalities.

The infantry battalions of most major belligerents were taken out of the line for retraining at regular intervals. The catastrophic level of casualties made this essential: battalions often had to be flooded with new recruits to bring them back up to strength. When British battalions were withdrawn to the rear, their refresher training often took place at central depots, under instructors based there rather

This is one of the thousands of Lewis guns captured by the Germans and modified to fire German 7.92 mm ammunition. The Musketen *battalions replaced their Madsens with Lewis guns at the end of 1916, and the machine gun companies of many stormtroop battalions retained captured Lewis guns even after a German light machine gun became available. (Pattern Room Collection)*

The MG '08 was too cumbersome to serve as an offensive weapon, but since the German army had shown such little interest in light machine guns before the war, the soldiers had to make do with it. Germans attacking at Verdun tried to push their MG '08s forward, leading to an intensive machine gun battle in the ruined village of Fleury. (Private collection)

than under their own officers. French infantry were also trained by officers seconded from the General Staff. However, German infantry remained under the control of their own officers all the time, including training periods behind the lines. In both World Wars, the German Army ensured that its private soldiers had the strongest possible bond between them and their regiment. Each regiment was recruited from a particular town or district, and a small cadre of officers and NCOs stayed there at the outbreak of war, ready to train the new recruits. Throughout the war, officers and NCOs from the regiment would return to the depot to supervise the training of new personnel. Returned wounded would be posted back to their old unit, returning to familiar faces.

The pre-war training of the German infantry was second to none. The veterans of the British Expeditionary Force may have been individually superior in many respects, but there were only six divisions of them. In August 1914 the German Army put four million men into the field. This was a tremendous asset that lasted Imperial Germany well into 1917. By then, many senior commanders were lamenting the end of the pre-war army, Ludendorff likening the German infantry of 1917 to a militia.

However, although the overall quality of the battalions may have declined through the horrendous losses on the Somme, the German infantry remained better trained than all its opponents. Even by 1918 between a quarter and a third of the German frontline infantry were pre-war trained.[8] Few British infantry companies had more than one or two individuals with any pre-war experience by then. French infantry battalions no doubt had more, but their pre-war training was of little relevance: the elbow-to-elbow charges persistently attempted in 1915 simply gave German machine guns an unmissable target.

German infantry officers received new training as well as their men. In the autumn of 1916 the Germans began to develop new defensive tactics, mainly as a response to the terrible power of the British artillery unleashed on the Somme. The traditional policy of packing the frontline with troops and not yielding an inch had cost the Germans dearly. From September company commanders were sent on month-long courses at training areas just behind the lines. There they studied the new, elastic defences that were to prove so effective in 1917.

Comprehensive retraining began a second time in the winter of 1917/18. Infantrymen received extra training in rifle shooting – a skill that had been lost by

all armies on the Western Front – and took part in endless route marches. By February 1918 battalions in the attack divisions were marching as far as 60 km a day – the same sort of breakneck speed demanded of the German infantry in 1914.[9] By maintaining such a relentless pace, the Germans gave the Italians no time to recover after their frontline was broken at Caporetto. However, the burden on the infantrymen had increased beyond all reason. A critical shortage of horses – and an almost complete dearth of motor transport – meant that artillery batteries had to make do with only four horses per gun, and at least half the infantry machine gun companies had to travel on foot.

The initial assault in March 1918 enjoyed the benefit of thorough rehearsal. Stormtroop battalions practised attacking full-scale models of their real objectives. Officers and senior NCOs had accurate aerial photographs to plan from. Live ammunition was used wherever possible, sometimes with unpredictable results:

'I made practice attacks with the company on complicated trench systems, with live grenades, in order to turn to account the lessons of the Cambrai battle . . . we had some casualties . . . A machine gunner of my company shot the commanding officer of another unit off his horse, while he was reviewing some troops. Fortunately the wound was not fatal.' [10]

The tactical manual they employed showed that the training role of the stormtroops was now complete. The 1918 edition of the German infantry training manual was effectively a stormtroopers' handbook. There was no mention of dedicated assault units within the battalion – all German infantrymen were supposed to be trained in that way. The infantry squad was now the prime tactical unit, and where earlier editions had included diagrams showing long skirmish lines, there were now symbols representing rifle squads or machine gun or mortar teams. Six of the 18 squads in a company were designated light machine gun squads.

ORGANISATION

There was no standard organisation among the stormtroop detachments created in 1915/16. Most were simply infantry companies with a few added heavy weapons. Only with the establishment of army-level assault battalions throughout the west did a general structure emerge. The stormtroop battalions formed in December 1916 consisted of:

- Headquarters: 10 officers and 32 men (although some were larger).
- 4 assault companies of about 4 officers and 120 other ranks.

Left: Shock troops implement the new skills of trench warfare over 'live firing' trenches at Sedan, August 1917. (IMW)

Austrian and German soldiers draw hot rations on the Italian front, where stormtroopers lead the demolition of the Italian army in October 1917. Stormtroopers enjoyed better rations than line battalions, and spent less time in the frontline trenches, where hot meals were a rarity. (IWM)

- 1 or 2 machine gun companies, each originally of 4 officers, 85 men and 6 machine guns, but expanded to 135 men and 12 machine guns during 1917.
- 1 flamethrower platoon of between 4 and 8 man-pack flamethrowers.
- 1 infantry gun battery of between 4 and 6 7.62 cm guns manned by about 80 men.
- 1 mortar company with 2 officers, about 100 other ranks and eight 7.6 cm mortars.

This formation included up to 1,400 officers and men, and was the basis of German infantry organisation during World War II. The number of infantry companies could vary from one to five of *Sturmbataillon Rohr*. Their strength varied too: Rohr's companies were over 200 strong, and those of the 3rd *Jäger-Sturmbataillon* had 263. Compared to a standard infantry regiment, a stormtrooper battalion included many more heavy weapons.

German line regiments consisted of three battalions, each about 800 strong and organised as follows:
- Battalion Headquarters.
- 3 infantry companies.
- 1 machine gun company of between 6 and 12 MG '08s.
- 1 mortar detachment of 4 light (7.6 cm) mortars.
- 1 signalling detachment with 8 battery-operated signal lamps.

Each infantry company consisted of three platoons, each divided into four 18-man sections. The latter were further sub-divided into two squads, each of one corporal and eight privates. This, the *Gruppe*, was the smallest unit, and was originally only an administrative arrangement that served no tactical purpose. The advent of light machine guns and the new tactics changed this for ever. As noted above, during 1917 each company received three MG '08/15s and many had at least six of them by the end of the year. The signalling detachments operated under the direction of the divisional signalling regiment; their largest lamps could be seen at up to 3,000 metres in daylight.

German battalions tended to be weaker in manpower, but sometimes stronger in heavy weapons. The 5th Grenadier regiment defending the Menin road in September 1917 was typical, occupying an 800-yard front with one battalion in the outpost zone, one in support and one in reserve. Companies averaged two officers, ten NCOs and 68 of other ranks. The regiment's heavy weapons comprised 35 MG '08s, 32 MG '08/15s and 12 light mortars. The

An MG '08/15 team in action during the battle of Champagne, April 1917. As German infantry companies received more light machine guns, platoons began to subdivide into 'gun groups' and 'rifle groups', capable of independent fire and movement. (IWM)

Dead Germans found in the British wire after a night raid near Givenchy. The stormtroop battalions specialised in trench raids, often breaking up 'live and let live' arrangements which sometimes developed on quieter sectors of the front. (Private collection)

280 men in the foremost battalion were caught by the British bombardment on 20 September and only 20 survived to surrender.

Assault battalions were often divided into company-size battlegroups and sent to undertake special missions in support of line infantry divisions. For example, on 21 March 1918 the 3rd *Jäger-Sturmbataillon* was split into four: one infantry company, one flamethrower platoon and two infantry guns were assigned to the 79th Reserve division; one company, a flamethrower platoon, two infantry guns, two mortars and a machine gun company went to the 50th Reserve division; a similar-sized force went to the 18th division; and one company and four mortars were held in reserve by the 2nd army.

FIGHTING SPIRIT

World War I imposed an unprecedented psychological burden on frontline soldiers. Battles were no longer fought and won in a few days, but lasted for weeks and months. Men no longer fought a visible foe: the infantrymen of both sides buried themselves in the earth to avoid the pitiless hail of projectiles. It

was a war of men against machines; flesh against steel. The battlefield doubled as a burial ground, with human remains frequently disinterred by shellfire as fast as they could be shovelled away. There was no martial glory for infantry. They never stood triumphant on a battlefield abandoned by the enemy, nor did they march into conquered cities; the frontlines hardly moved. All they could do was to endure.

The stormtroopers were different: unlike ordinary infantrymen, they spent little time on the defensive, skulking in filthy trenches. Arriving at the front by lorry, they would filter into position after dusk and make a sudden assault on the enemy lines. By dawn, they would be on their way back to base, taking their prisoners with them – and leaving the infantry in that sector to face the inevitable Allied retaliatory bombardment. They were certainly used to shatter the 'live and let live' system (the informal truce arrangements sometimes arrived at by German and Allied infantry) and they were conscious of their status. They wore customised uniforms, carried whole bags full of grenades, and tucked coshes and daggers into their belts. Like fighter pilots and U-Boat crew, the stormtroopers became romantic figures to the German popular press – heroes to be

emulated. The German war bond posters of 1914–16 featured a medieval knight, representing the German soldier; in 1917 the knight was replaced by a lantern-jawed, steely-eyed hero in a *Stahlhelm*, a gas-mask dangling from his neck and a bag of grenades at the ready. This was the new face of the German warrior.

Stormtroop battalions also served to bolster the fighting spirit of the rest of the army. To become a stormtrooper was the aspiration of many keen young recruits, and if the stormtroopers' trench raids sometimes upset the frontline units in one sector, the reports of their deeds made welcome reading for German soldiers elsewhere. Men who had spent harrowing weeks under intensive Allied shellfire, unable to hit back, were heartened to hear of the stormtroops' exploits. Their raids were not just re-ported in Germany, but featured heavily in trench newspapers, one of which was even called *Der Stosstrupp* and carried a regular section entitled *Stosstruppgeist* (stormtrooper spirit).[11]

As the Royal Navy's blockade of Germany began to take effect, so the German civilian population ran short of food as inflation eroded families' incomes. After the privations of the dreadful 'turnip winter' of 1916, anti-war feeling within Germany led to parlia-mentary demands for peace and to industrial unrest. Soldiers could not be isolated from this: while the army could censor their letters home, it could not edit the replies. Morale suffered as news from Ger-many filtered through the ranks. It had some curious side-effects, such as soldiers hacking off their jack-boot heels and posting them home to family members short of footwear. (The soldiers then drew new boots from company stores.)

The morale of the stormtroopers was clearly higher than that of some units of the regular army. This division was formalised in the reorganisation during the winter of 1917/18: the young, fit and keen were gathered into the 'attack divisions', and the less motivated were left behind. In the Kaiser's Battle, this helped the Germans break through, but meant that casualties were concentrated among their best soldiers. The very success of this attack exposed the German High Command as liars: German propa-ganda had claimed that the enemy were on their knees, that Britain was being strangled by the U-Boats, but the size and content of the vast British supply dumps that were overrun that March told another story altogether: cases of coffee, chocolate, cigarettes – and the company rum. This proved all too tempting for hungry infantrymen in 1918, and looting slowed down the German advance. At the same time, even the least reflective stormtrooper became aware that he faced an uphill struggle. One soldier questioned in his diary whether the British were trying to make everything they could out of copper and brass, just to taunt the Germans, who were so short of vital metals.

LOGISTICS

Supplying troops in the trenches was fraught with difficulty. Supplies from the rear were likely to be unreliable, 80 troops going into the frontline took at least five days' rations with them. Small cookers fired by solidified alcohol were used to warm food in the trenches, and large vaccum flasks were provided so that hot coffee or soup could be carried up. Ration parties were dispatched whenever hostile fire permit-ted, delivering food from ration depots established close to the positions. They were frequently delayed by enemy artillery fire or got lost in the pitch dark-

German 10 cm guns in position near the river Sereth during the invasion of Rumania. Three of the four Jäger battalions earmarked for conversion to stormtroop units in 1916 were rushed to the Eastern Front instead. After fighting in Rumania, they rejoined the Alpine Corps for the Caporetto offensive. (US National Archives)

ness, so the drinks were often cold by the time the soldiers received them.

Since most water in northern France and Belgium was undrinkable, the German Army was forced to organise local drinking-water systems. Pipes were laid from existing waterworks or mains and new wells were dug and pumps installed. Breweries, sugar factories and other suitable buildings were converted to water treatment plants. Drinking water was piped into villages as close to the frontline as possible, and sometimes as far forward as the support trenches. This system broke down on the Somme, when the sheer weight of Allied artillery fire cut the pipes. The Germans resorted to mineral water, taking over existing factories and providing reserves of carbonated water close to the front. When soldiers entered the line, they took two water bottles and as many bottles of carbonated water as they could find.

The 1916-pattern Granatenwerfer weighed 16 kg, the steel platform another 24 kg, and was an awkward shape to carry unless dismantled. It fired its 1.85 kg grenade to a range of 50–300 m. The 1916 German organisation was 12 grenade throwers per infantry regiment. (Pattern Room Collection)

Food Supplies

In 1914, German field service daily rations consisted of:
- 750 g bread or 400 g egg biscuit or 500 g field biscuit
- 375 g fresh meat or 200 g preserved meat
- 125–250 g vegetables or 1,500 g potatoes or 60 g dried vegetables
- 25 g coffee or 3 g tea
- 20 g sugar
- 25 g salt

The meat ration was gradually reduced, falling to 350 g at the end of 1915, and to 288 g by mid-1916, when one meatless day a week was introduced. In October 1916 it was cut to 250 g. Portions of preserved meat were cut to 150 g. Soldiers not actually in the frontline had only 200 g of meat from June 1916.

Company commanders could order a daily ration of a half a litre of beer, a quarter litre of wine or 125 ml of brandy, rum or arrack. The daily tobacco ration was two cigars or cigarettes or 30 g of pipe tobacco.

In the frontline trenches, soldiers often had to rely on their iron ration. They carried at least one iron ration, and usually more. It consisted of:

- 250 g biscuit
- 200 g preserved meat or bacon
- 150 g preserved vegetables
- 25 g coffee
- 25 g salt

German infantry on the Western Front were compelled to abandon their trenches during the major battles of 1916. Their splendid deep trenches provided excellent protection, but they were conspicuous targets. Once British 9.2-in. howitzers obtained their range, the bunkers became death traps and the infantry was forced to fight from shell craters instead. Lurking in the surreal landscape carved out

A French 120 mm gun in action on the Aisne: after their unsuccessful offensive of 1915, the French Army relied on its heavy artillery to pulverise the German positions before any infantry attack took place. This tactic enabled small advances to take place, but no breakthrough could be accomplished because it took so long to move the guns forward. (Private collection)

by the guns, the infantry were much harder for Allied forward artillery observers to locate. But it brought new hardships: ration parties failed to reach many units or took so long to find the soldiers that the food was ruined. Wounded men could no longer be evacuated along relatively safe communication trenches; instead they faced a hazardous journey across the wasteland, balanced on the shoulders of their comrades. More often than not, they had to wait until last light before any such movement could be attempted.

MEDICAL SERVICES

Each German infantry battalion had two medical officers, four medical NCOs (one per company) and 16 stretcher bearers. The latter wore the red cross and were officially non-combatants. In the trenches companies usually established a medical aid post just behind the fire trench. The regimental aid post was in the second support trench and usually in dug-outs or cellars designed to accommodate 30 wounded men each. They were provided with electric lighting, extra rations and stockpiles of dressings. The regimental aid post was staffed by three battalion medical

officers and eight stretcher bearers from the divisional bearer company (*Sanitätskompagnie*). A wounded soldier who required more treatment than the regimental aid post could offer was evacuated to a 'wagon rendezvous' (*Wagenhalteplatz*): a group of dug-outs about 4,000 metres behind the regimental aid post and manned by personnel from the divisional bearer company. Hot drinks and food could be provided here, and this post was connected by telephone to the main dressing station further to the rear. Wagons kept here were sent forward under cover of darkness to help the bearers bring back wounded soldiers.

The wounded were then evacuated to the main dressing station, usually situated in a shell-proof shelter, probably in a village about 10 km behind the frontline trenches. Walking wounded were assembled into groups at the wagon rendezvous and sent back together. Wounded men were given medical cards that showed whether they were able to walk, were fit to be transported to the rear, or were too badly injured to move. Soldiers found at the main dressing station without a card or other authorisation were sent back to their unit. Because there were never enough stretcher bearers, wounded men were often carried back by their comrades, but every attempt was made to prevent stragglers slipping back to the aid posts and staying there.

Evacuation Problems

Evacuating a wounded man was fraught with peril. Even if a stretcher party was not deliberately targeted by the enemy, there was more than enough random machine gun and artillery fire to strike them down. Gustav Ebelhauser helped carry back his friend across the battle-scarred landscape of the Somme:

'Every crater, every crevice, every hole unfolded new and more horrible pictures of death. One man they passed had his carcass torn to pieces, and was missing his head ... Further on their feet dipped into the belly of another, causing the bowels to burst from the mutilated body.'

They reached the aid post, where Ebelhauser's comrade died on the operating table.[12]

Most casualties – perhaps as many as 80 per cent – were caused by artillery. The shells burst into large chunks of razor-sharp iron that inflicted ghastly injuries. Although these soldiers often had the ben-

German dead lie in a shellscrape, struck by Allied artillery fire. Forced to evacuate their trenches by accurate heavy shellfire, the

Germans fought from shell craters, where they were still vulnerable to air burst shrapnel. (US National Archives)

efit of anaesthetic, it was difficult to evacuate them from a battlefield so often reduced to a sea of mud-filled craters. The sheer number of wounded frequently swamped the available medical facilities, condemning many men to a miserable death because they could not be treated in time.

Gas Attacks

By introducing poison gas, the Germans added a new dimension of horror to the battlefield, and if the Allies were slower to find such an evil use for their chemical industry, they soon made up for lost time. The French had a working gas shell by 1916; Haig badgered the British government for gas shell too, and received a limited quantity for the latter stages of the Somme battle. By 1917 German soldiers were subjected to regular chemical attack, with the British specialising in saturation bombardments. One such attack struck St Quentin on 19 March 1918, just as the town filled up with troops for the German offensive: 3,000 drums of chlorine gas were fired from the British lines at 10 p.m., submerging the buildings in a thick greenish-white cloud. Respirators were of little help: the gas was in such concentration that no oxygen came through the filters. Fresh troops entering the area the next morning found the streets full of men coughing up the bloody remains of their lungs. One NCO from the 16th Bavarian reserve regiment would survive the Kaiser's Battle the following week, but end the war hospitalised after a mustard gas attack – Adolf Hitler recovered from his injuries but refused to authorise the use of chemical weapons in World War II. He believed the Allies would retaliate with even more deadly nerve agents than the scientists of the Third Reich could provide.

Disease

Until 1914, disease usually killed more soldiers than did the enemy. The first major conflict in which bullets claimed more lives than germs was the Russo-Japanese war of 1904/5. During World War I soldiers of all armies on the Western Front experienced the same phenomenon – partly due to improved medical care, and partly due to the unprecedented carnage on the battlefield. The single most important medical achievement of the German Army was to shield itself and Germany from the typhus epidemic that inflicted such terrible suffering on the Serbs and Russians. Frequent de-lousing of their own men and enemy POWs kept the disease out of central and western Europe, while it literally decimated the Serbian nation.

In October 1918 Germany was struck by the worst influenza epidemic of the 20th century. The 'Spanish Flu' was a virulent infection that struck across the whole world in the late summer of that year; it afflicted America, Europe and Asia simultaneously, but its effects were maximised in Europe, where civilian populations were already weakened by years of poor diet. Few German families escaped the soaring fever and hacking coughs that characterised the infection, and by November there were 400 deaths a day in Hamburg alone. When the disease vanished – as suddenly as it had come – it left 400,000 Germans dead. More people died in the latter half of 1918 than in the entire war. Militarily, it was the last straw for the German Army – the end to the High Command's hopes of prolonging the struggle. Even the most die-hard stormtroopers could not fight with a temperature of 40 degrees (104°F).

The total number of German casualties during World War I will never be known exactly. It was controversial at the time: the High Command had resorted to deliberate falsification and many records were lost during the war. Approximately two million German soldiers died: roughly one in six of those mobilised. While in Britain the casualties sustained under Haig's command have attracted vocal criticism since the 1920s, it is worth noting that Germany's most successful offensive in the west, the great breakthrough in March 1918 and the subsequent

Stormtroopers training at Sedan, May 1917. Note how one soldier carries a massive pair of wire cutters, one has a shovel and the soldier on the far left has a stick grenade at the ready. (IWM)

NCO, Sturmbataillion, May 1916

A

B

Returning from a trench raid

Stormtrooper training, Sedan 1917

C

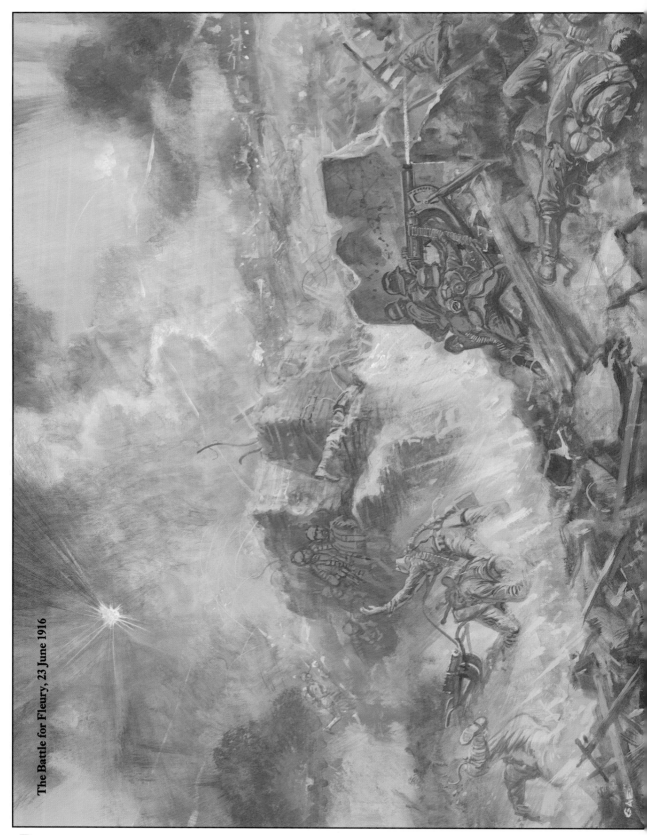

The Battle for Fleury, 23 June 1916

D

Wurttembergisches Gebirgs-Bataillion, Caporetto,
October 1917

E

F   **Guard Pioneer flamethrower team, Fort Douamont, May 1916**

**Helmets and insignia
(see plate commentary)**

G

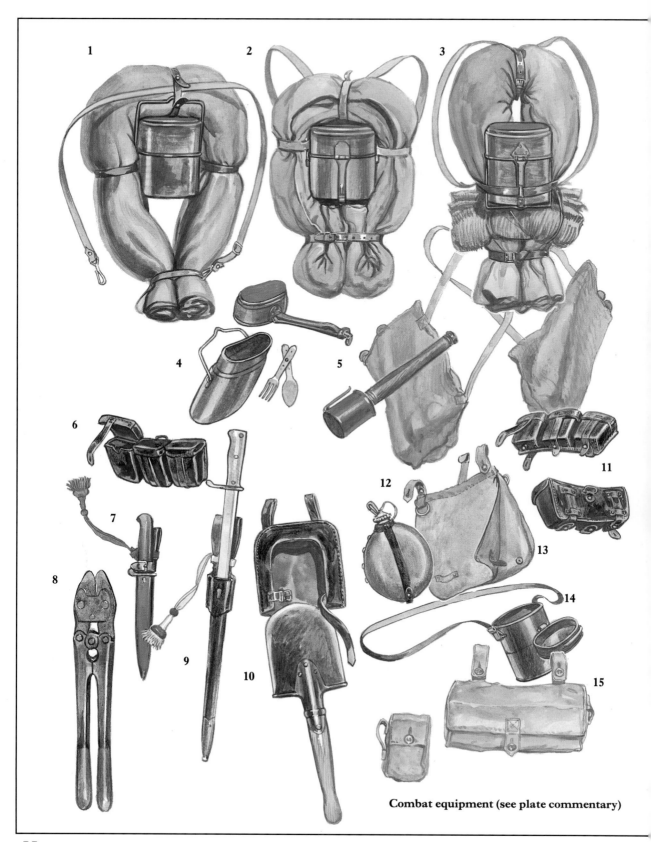

Combat equipment (see plate commentary)

H

3rd Jager-Sturmbataillion counter-attacks at Cambria

I

NCO, Angriffsdivision, March 1918

J

Stormtroopers capture a British battery, March 1918

K

Freikorps unit in street
fighting, bavaria 1919

L

assaults between April and June, cost the German Army 125,000 killed in action, 738,000 wounded and 104,000 missing or captured – a total of 963,000 casualties.

COMBAT TACTICS

Prior to 1914, German infantry training was almost exclusively devoted to offensive tactics. Yet there was no consensus on how to attack across a battlefield dominated by quick-firing artillery, bolt-action rifles and machine guns. It seemed obvious that infantry needed to spread out to survive, but from the 1880s there was a sharp reaction against open order tactics, generals remembered the chaos that had ensued in many of the battles of 1870. At Gravelotte, for example, skirmishers became pinned down, unable to go forward or back, and whole battalions dissolved into disorderly mobs. Some officers came to believe that while closer formations might suffer more casualties in the short term, they were easier to control, and by retaining mobility, they would lose fewer men in the long term. This school of thought was rather discredited by the Boer wars, when British infantry were frequently pinned down by long-range Mauser fire.

In the first years of the 20th century, German infantry reverted to widely spaced lines of skirmishers – 'Boer tactics' – only to return to closer formations as the difficulties of controlling such scattered units became apparent. An 80-man platoon spread over a 300 m front was impossible for its commander to manage. The commanders of the German corps districts had a free hand in the training of their men, which explains the patchy performance of German infantry in 1914: some divisions operated in thin skirmish lines, others came on in dense masses as if machine guns had never been invented. This lack of cohesion was punished with bloody finality in 1914: battalions attempting to close with the enemy in columns of platoons were cut to pieces. Even against the questionable marksmanship of the French and Russian armies, dense formations usually failed. Against the BEF they were nothing short of suicide: witness the bloody repulse of the Prussian Foot Guards at Ypres.

Attacks with limited objectives

After the failure of the Schlieffen Plan, the German Army remained on the defensive in the west for the whole of 1915. Throughout that year the French Army expended hundreds of thousands of men trying to break through the German trench lines. British attempts in the spring and autumn were equally

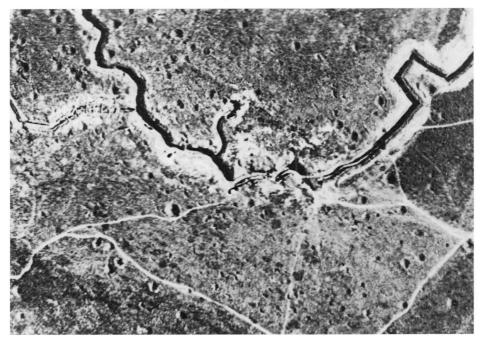

Trenches were clearly visible from the air, and Allied observer aircraft were constantly above the German lines, directing artillery fire against them. German wireless stations monitored their signals, and could give some warning when a position was about to be shelled. (US National Archives)

disastrous. However, the Germans were not entirely passive: divisional commanders frequently ordered 'attacks with limited objectives' (*Angriffe mit begrenzten Ziele*) to secure important ground or deny key terrain to the enemy. Pre-war German doctrine dictated that the methods by which such attacks were achieved were the responsibility of the local commanders, unlike their French counterparts, who were snowed under with tactical instructions from the General Staff.

By employing all the pre-war tactics of siege warfare German infantry were frequently able to seize French or British positions. The German Army had a far higher proportion of howitzers in its field artillery batteries, and this proved to be a crucial advantage. High-trajectory fire was much more effective against trenches than the flat-shooting field guns that made up the majority of British and French batteries. Howitzers, hand grenades and mortars enabled the German infantry to capture the frontline enemy trenches, and helped hold them against a counter-attack. The vital high ground of Pilckem Ridge, the scene of their heavy losses in 1914, was taken by the Germans in April 1915 with the aid of 150 tons of chlorine gas, one attack with limited objectives that succeeded beyond expectation. Yet neither the artillery nor the new terror weapon enabled the infantry to make a major breakthrough.

'The Hell of Verdun'

Attacking infantry faced two main obstacles – barbed wire and machine gun nests – and they had little time to deal with them. Defending artillery was likely to bring down a heavy barrage in No-Man's Land the moment signal flares sailed into the air from the enemy trenches. When, in February 1916, the German Army returned to the offensive and attacked Verdun, the assault was spearheaded by stormtroops and Pioneers. While German artillery batteries suppressed the French guns with new gas shell, detachments of *sturmtruppen* charged over the top to open gaps in the French wire. The concrete machine gun posts that dotted the gently sloping hills on the east bank of the Meuse were attacked by the flamethrowers of Reddemann's 3rd Guard Pioneer battalion. Other stormtroop units raced to lob grenades into the French trenches. In some sectors, mountain guns with large steel shields were manoeuvred out of the German frontline trenches to engage concrete strongpoints in direct fire.

The stormtroopers were followed by the line infantry, swarming forward in skirmish lines reminiscent of 1914. They occupied the French positions, overrunning any surviving bands of defenders. Succeeding waves of infantry brought forward the MG '08s and box after box of ammunition to defeat the inevitable French counter-attacks.

In October 1917 the Alpine Corps spearheaded the German offensive at Caporetto, the most comprehensive battlefield victory of World War I. The breakthrough was complete, 30,000 Italian troops were killed and 300,000 surrendered. (US National Archives)

Right: A German 7.7 cm field gun at full recoil: the gun is mounted on a low carriage with small wheels to make it a smaller target. 50 of the Nahkampf-batterien (close-range batteries) formed in 1917 used 7.7 cm guns converted in this manner. (US National Archives)

The initial success at Verdun was not sustained after the first week. The French rushed in fresh infantry divisions and countless batteries of artillery – and German casualties mounted. Attacking German regiments continued to organise detachments of stormtroops to lead their assaults, but it proved harder and harder to coordinate the infantry rushes with the artillery support. Once beyond their original frontline, the Germans were no longer working from accurate maps and aerial photographs. The French did not occupy such obvious positions, and many attacks came unstuck in hidden belts of barbed wire, or were decimated by previously concealed machine guns.

The initial German infantry attacks were supported by 1,600 guns, two-thirds of which were heavy howitzers. The devastation wrought by this unprecedented artillery concentration was incredible, but in a perverse way it led to a strengthening of the French defences. French infantry learned that digging proper trenches merely offered the German gunners a clear target. In the moonscape battlefield of Verdun, the defenders began to fight from shell holes, improvised positions within the tangled wreckage of the forests, and fortified basements among the ruined villages. To counter this more effective defence in depth, stormtroops tried to press on regardless of what was happening to their flanks, trusting to the succeeding waves of infantry to follow their progress. German artillery began to employ a 'rolling barrage', dropping a curtain of shells ahead of the infantry, although in practice the barrage often moved on too fast. As stormtroop detachments penetrated the network of French positions, they inevitably bypassed some of them: and this was the origin of 'infiltration tactics'.

Defending on the Somme

The Verdun offensive was called off in the summer of 1916 when the British Army launched its long-awaited offensive on the Somme. Britain has never really recovered from this – its first experience of continental warfare in the industrial age, but for the Germans it was equally disagreeable. For German infantry, obliged to sit in darkened bunkers reverberating under the tons of high explosive, the Somme was a nightmare. British accounts might praise the German fortifications, frequently remarking that the

deep underground shelters were impervious to all but a direct hit, but this was small consolation when the monstrous guns of the Royal Garrison Artillery did score direct hits. Whole platoons were buried alive. Counter-attacks broke down as battalions lost half their men before they reached the start line.

'The English bombardment kept increasing in intensity at the turn of each hour. Even when night settled over the mutilated fields of France, there had been no let up ... For three more days and nights it was for Ebelhauser and his comrades nothing short of hell on earth. Fire came crashing down from all directions ... turning shell hole after shell hole into open and silent tombs. How many soldiers lay buried there, soldiers whose bodies would never be found? The earth shook night and day ... The few remaining defenders of this section of the Western Front had become nothing more than crawling animals, seeking refuge in ever fresh-made holes. They slid from one crater to another in vain search for food as well as protection. But neither could be found.'[13]

When warm summer weather dried the liquid mud of the Ypres battlefield, it brought new hazards. Human remains attracted a plague of flies by day and rats by night. (Private collection)

If the Somme left some officers and men in the British Army rather less confident in the judgement of their senior commanders, German infantry experienced similar doubts in theirs. Infantry regiments followed the unbending Prussian tradition of 'Halten, was zu halten ist' ('Hold on to whatever can be held'). The frontline was packed with troops, offering a prime target to the British guns and their apparently limitless reserves of ammunition.[14] Officers who wished to do otherwise were given little incentive: some commanders who failed to regain lost ground were relieved of their command. General von Falkenhayn's words were of little comfort: *'The enemy must not be allowed to advance except over corpses.'* German infantrymen did resist to the end, with the result that by August 1916 the German Army had lost as many men on the Somme in two months as in six months' fighting at Verdun. By the end of the battle, 138 German divisions had fought there, as opposed to the 75 that were engaged at Verdun; few of them had more than 3,000 infantrymen – less than half their original strength.

Like the French at Verdun, the Germans eventually found it impossible to maintain a proper frontline on the Somme. They resorted to fighting from shell holes, occupying their front with mutually supporting outposts and machine gun nests. The bulk of the infantry were withdrawn several thousand metres, but stood ready to counter-attack. Throughout the Somme battle, the German infantry launched counter-attacks by day and night. Most were in battalion or regimental strength, although they did deliver an all-out effort against Delville Wood, prepared by four days' heavy shelling. The German High Command attributed their reverses on the Somme to the lack of depth of their defences, the excessive concentration of infantry in the frontline and the Allies' superiority in artillery and aircraft. The latter advantage was keenly noticed by the infantrymen:

'*French aeroplanes circled above our position and flew over our heads towards the base lines; but there was no sign of a German plane. We did not like our air force in any case, because of their swagger, and now we cursed them more than ever.*'[15]

It was extremely demoralising to have Allied observer aircraft circling overhead. The Germans monitored the aircraft's radio transmissions, and were able to warn artillery batteries when their position had been compromised, enabling the gunners to get into their dug-outs or even evacuate the battery. But there was nowhere for the infantry to go, and no way to communicate with them quickly enough anyway.

Elastic defence

The Germans formalised their new defensive system during the winter of 1916/17. According to their new instructions for the defensive battle (*Führung der Abwehrschlact*) issued in December 1916, a forward zone of about 500–1,000 m was held by outposts only. This would keep back Allied patrols and disrupt the first stage of an attack. The main line of resistance was behind this – usually sited on a reverse slope, with up to three lines of trenches. Behind the trenches, stretching back for up to 2,000 m, were a series of well-camouflaged concrete strongpoints, arranged in a rough checkerboard pattern to provide mutual support. This was where the Germans intended to fight their defensive battle – out of view of Allied artillery observers and in plain view of their own. Waiting behind the main line of resistance were the German counter-attack forces, poised to attack

Dismounted German cavalry counter-attack under cover of their machine guns, September 1918. Lack of mounted cavalry restricted the German success in March, when the stormtroopers were able to break through Allied defences, but not to pursue the beaten defenders. (IWM)

the enemy just as they lost impetus; with their offensive stalled by heavy artillery and machine gun fire, Allied infantry could be overwhelmed by a judiciously timed counter-attack.

The new German defensive tactics placed great emphasis on counter-attacks, particularly those delivered from the flanks. Just as on the Russian Front in World War II where the Germans allowed Soviet tanks to break through, only to destroy them by a pincer movement, so in World War I the Germans wiped out whole brigades of British and French infantry by isolating them within the German defences. Attacking from the flanks, the Germans recaptured their forward positions, at the same time isolating Allied attackers who had penetrated to the German second- or third-line trenches. Unable to communicate with their artillery or bring forward ammunition, the would-be attackers were annihilated.

The emphasis on infantry counter-attacks helped develop stormtroop tactics further. Aggressive infantry were the key to the German success, and during the defensive battles of 1917, the German infantry began to perfect the methods they would use in their own offensive the following spring.

However, the defensive battles were not without cost: the *Materialschlacht* (battle of material) pitted German infantry against the industrial might of the British and French empires. After their profligate expenditure of infantry in 1914/15, the French settled on the systematic pulverisation of German trenches by massed heavy artillery and then occupied the lifeless ruins that remained. The British followed suit. At Messines, 2,266 British guns delivered 144,000 tons of explosive in support of a limited offensive that began with the detonation of massive mines underneath the German trenches.

The barrage that opened the great British offensive in Flanders was even worse than on the Somme. While the name of Passchendaele evokes a particular chill in British hearts, defending the Ypres sector in 1917 was a uniquely ghastly business for the German infantry, despite their advanced tactical ideas. 'The 'Hell of Verdun' was surpassed and the Flanders battle was called 'the greatest martyrdom of the World War'. There were no trenches and no shelters except the few concrete blockhouses:

'In the water-filled craters cowered the defenders without shelter from weather, hungry and cold, abandoned without pause to overwhelming artillery fire.' [16]

A typical barbed wire entanglement which protected the Hindenburg Line. German engineers laid vast belts of wire, which were supposed to channel attacking infantry into machine gun killing zones. (Private collection)

Men Against Tanks

The battle of Cambrai began disastrously for the Germans, with whole units taking to their heels as hundreds of tanks ground over their positions. Tanks had not worried the Germans unduly until this encounter: despite General Sir Douglas Haig's urgent pleas for more armour, the Royal Tank Regiment could only attack in penny packets during 1916, and the first major attack by French armour in 1917 had met with utter defeat. Some 82 Schneiders and St. Armand tanks went into action on 16 April, but many got stuck trying to cross a landscape of lip-to-lip craters, and German artillery knocked them out one by one.

On the firm level ground at Cambrai, it was a different story. The massed tank attack achieved surprise, the thunderous noise of so many tank engines being drowned by low-flying British aircraft, and there was no preliminary artillery bombardment. Fortunately for the Germans, the tanks of 1917 were mechanically unreliable, and the number of operational vehicles dwindled rapidly; by the time the Germans launched their counter-attack ten days later, there were not enough tanks to stem it, let alone to mount another armoured offensive.

On 30 November it was the turn of the German air force to swoop low over the battlefield. For the

Stormtroopers of the German Naval division after the attack on the British bridgehead over the Yser, July 1917. The Naval Sturmabteilung *led the 1st and 2nd Marine regiments in an assault that overwhelmed the 1st Northamptonshire and* *2nd KRRC. Artillery support for this limited assault included 30 batteries of field guns, 12 of light howitzers, 16 of heavy howitzers, seven siege batteries, 10 Minenwerfer batteries and two (Naval) 24 cm guns. (IWM)*

first time in the war, German aircraft were used in close support of the infantry:

'Preceded by patrols, the Germans advanced at 7 a.m. in small columns bearing many light machine guns and, in some cases, flamethrowers. From overhead, low-flying aircraft . . . bombed and machine gunned the British defenders, causing further casualties and, especially, distraction at the critical moment. Nevertheless, few posts appear to have been attacked from the front, the assault sweeping in between to envelop them from flanks and rear.'[17]

The phrase 'infiltration tactics' has been widely used to describe the German infantry's new offensive technique. It is therefore something of a surprise to find no mention of 'infiltration' in German sources. The expression is an understandable description of what the Allies thought was happening, but it was not the whole story. The new tactics were first encountered by the French after the failure of Gen-

An M1880 10.5 howitzer captured by the British in Mametz Wood, August 1916. During the battle of the Somme the German army launched several hundred local counter-attacks, frequently led by regimental and divisional stormtroop detachments. (US National Archives)

eral Nivelle's offensive in April 1917. German coun-ter-attacks were sudden, and very violent.

'They were heralded by very accurate artillery fire concentrated on the point of attack. The ground the Germans intended recapturing would be turned into a field of smoke and flame under a roaring, screeching sky that seemed about to collapse, forcing down the heads of the defenders; trenches would rock and cave under the violence of the explosions, then the air would buzz as the steel wasps of German machine gun bullets came over . . . Suddenly the range would lengthen and, looming out of the smoke of the last explosions, shadowy forms would rush forward, gesticulating wildly, enemy soldiers throw-ing grenades.' [18]

What the Allies persisted in calling 'infiltration tactics' was described by the Germans as 'coordina-tion' – of all the different weapons now employed by an infantry battalion. This is perhaps best illustrated by an example of small-unit tactics from the battle of Cambrai. On 30 November, the 2nd Battalion, 109th Infantry regiment, had penetrated the British front but was halted by machine gun fire approximately 500 m from Gonnelieu. Three separate machine gun positions were pinning the regiment down, and it proved impossible to communicate with the support-ing artillery – a familiar problem on the battlefields of World War I. The 5th company of the 110th Infantry

regiment had been following in reserve, and was now pushed forward to attack the main machine gun post that was blocking any further progress. Adjacent British positions were taken under fire by the regi-mental machine gun company, and a *minenwerfer* was brought forward to a shell crater, and used to shell the 5th company's objective. German artillery fire finally came down, shelling the immediate rear of the British machine guns. Dividing into squads, the 5th company worked around the machine gun position, making a short rush from cover to cover each time the *minenwerfer* dropped a bomb on the British. A squad led by Sergeant Gersbach reached the old trenchline that led to the British machine gun, and bombed its way along the trench, lobbing grenades into each firing bay. The machine gun was captured and the advance of the 109th regiment could con-tinue. The whole operation, from the regimental commander ordering up the mortar and machine gun platoons to the storming of the trench took about two hours. Combined arms tactics were essential in order to achieve success.:

'The squad leader, supported by the fire of heavy infantry weapons and acting in conjunction with neigh-bouring rifle and machine gun squads, continues the attack from nest to nest, seeking always to strike the enemy resistance from the flank.' [19]

The Kaiser's Battle

By the time the stormtroops led the great German offensive of March 1918, German infantry tactics had changed beyond recognition. The smallest 'tactical brick' was now the infantry squad, itself divided into a 'gun group' of one MG '08/15 manned by two gunners and two ammunition carriers, and a 'rifle group' of between eight and ten men led by a corporal. Some other armies would take until the middle of World War II to accept this structure as the best way to achieve fire and manoeuvre within an infantry platoon.

Ludendorff's offensive was an all-or-nothing enterprise by which Imperial Germany would either achieve its war aims or be utterly destroyed. To this end, the stormtroops were ordered to push on at all costs. Whereas at Verdun they had gone firm on their objectives, which were then occupied by regular infantry, in 1918 they were to stop for nothing. They were to bypass those enemy positions that still held out, and keep advancing regardless of what was happening behind them or on their flanks. But this led to heavy losses during the first week of the offensive. Passing beyond the reach of German artillery, and leaving many of their own heavy weapons behind, the stormtroopers ran into enemy defences they could not overcome.

From March to June 1918 the stormtroop battalions led a succession of all-out attacks, and many were burned out in the process. They achieved unprecedented tactical victories, but enjoyed only local effects. In the end, the tactical excellence of the stormtroopers could not compensate for the political and strategic blindness of the German High Command. By holding out for unacceptable peace terms and concentrating on tactical warfare rather than grand strategy, they had condemned Germany to defeat. It was not the fault of the stormtroops; as one of their officers recorded:

Each German Corps headquarters was allocated a balloon detachment of between four and six observation balloons. One balloon communicated with the infantry divisional HQs, while the others were used for artillery observation. (US Army)

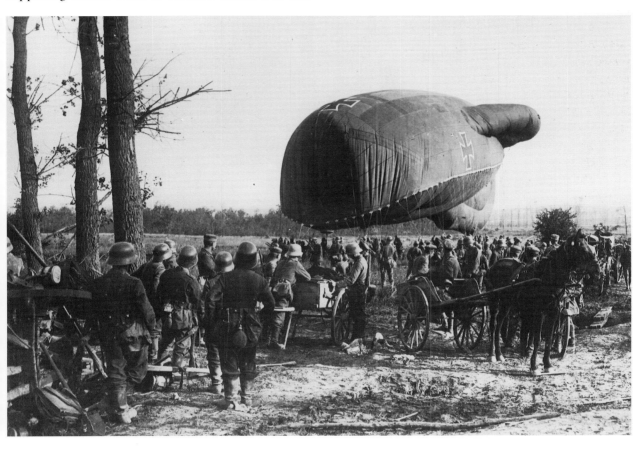

'*The brazen spirit of the attack, the spirit of Prussian infantry, swept through the massed troops . . . after forty-four months of hard fighting they threw themselves on the enemy with all the enthusiasm of August 1914. No wonder it needed a world in arms to bring such a storm-flood to a standstill.*'[20]

THE PLATES

A: NCO, *Sturmbataillon Rohr*, May 1916

A young veteran of Germany's first 'official' storm-trooper battalion observes the arrival of a new training cadre. On 15 May 1916 the Chief of the German General Staff, General Erich von Falkenhayn, ordered all armies on the Western Front to send groups of officers and NCOs to *Sturmbataillon Rohr* to receive training in stormtroop tactics. Rohr's battalion was serving at Verdun where it had spearheaded the initial German attack in February. Detachments from the battalion continued to lead attacks in this sector, while the bulk of the unit provided tactical training. The stormtroops were among the first to receive the new steel helmet, the *Stahlhelm*; during 1915 Rohr's men had tested both the helmet and other body armour including steel shields and breastplates. The stormtroops had discovered that ankle boots and puttees provided better support than the traditional jackboots, and their uniform would continue to diverge from that of the pre-war infantry.

B: Returning from a trench raid

A detachment of stormtroops returns through the German trenches after a night raid on the French lines. They bring some prisoners with them as they start the journey to their barracks in a safe rear area. The Germans garrisoning this section of the front regard the stormtroops with mixed feelings: they have struck a blow against the enemy, but they will be long gone when the French retaliate by bringing down a heavy artillery bombardment. The stormtroopers enjoyed massive artillery support themselves: a raid by perhaps 100 stormtroops might be aided by all the guns of a German infantry division – 15–20 batteries on a front engaged in heavy fighting. The artillery would isolate the target trench by shelling either side of it and bombarding all communication trenches leading to it. Joined by trench

Stormtroopers wait in their jumping-off trenches, ready to attack across the Sedan training area during 1917. The realism of their training exercises paid handsome dividends during the offensive of March 1918. (IWM)

A German 21 cm howitzer with slats on its wheels to reduce the recoil. Even with the spade trailer dug in and wedges under the wheels, the 5 tonne gun still leapt back nearly a metre when it fired. (US Army)

mortars, the heavy guns delivered a short but intense barrage on the target itself, just before the stormtroops went over the top. Other enemy trenches might be shelled at the same time in order to mislead the enemy as to the true objective of the raid.

C: Stormtrooper training, Sedan, autumn 1917

The Germans established a number of training areas around Sedan. Here, infantrymen posted to stormtroop battalions were taught the new skills developed on the battlefield by these elite assault units. NCOs sent to the stormtroop battalions assumed much greater responsibility, learning to lead small units themselves, rather than just providing support for their officers. One such NCO was Sergeant Joseph

'Sepp' Dietrich, who served with the 2nd Bavarian assault battlion in 1917. He transferred to a tank unit in 1918 and after the war rose from Hitler's bodyguard to SS Panzer commander.

Stormtrooper training was conducted in as realistic a manner as possible, with plentiful use of live ammunition. Raids on actual enemy trenches were launched after a very thorough study of the ground and following rehearsals over life-size mock-ups of the objective. Smoke was used to simulate gas (the stormtroopers frequently assaulted with the support of gas shell). Stormtroop tactics laid great emphasis on the cooperation of all weapons: rifles, machine guns, grenades, mortars, flamethrowers and artillery. Enemy fire was suppressed by the heavy weapons while the stormtroopers worked their way forward; at the last moment, the riflemen joined in, keeping the enemies' heads down as their comrades lobbed stick grenades over the parapet.

D: The Battle for Fleury, 23 June 1916

The German Alpine Corps evolved tactics very similar to those of the stormtroops. These elite mountain troops spearheaded the last major German offensive at Verdun, joining *Sturmbataillon Rohr* and the flamethrower teams of the 3rd Guard Pioneer regiment for an attack on the village of Fleury. The Bavarian Life Guard broke through to the village, only to find it heavily fortified, with French machine gun teams holding out in fortified cellars. The Bavarians brought forward their own heavy machine guns, and in desperate close quarter fighting, the Germans managed to capture the ruins. Here an MG '08 team keeps a French strongpoint under fire, while a team of bombers creep towards the enemy, stick grenades at the ready. Another MG '08 team arrives, dragging the machine gun forward with a leather harness. When the Allies first encountered this harness, it gave rise to the legend that German machine gunners were strapped to their guns. Despite their eventual success at Fleury, the MG '08 was too cumbersome to advance with attacking troops, and the Germans were behind the Allies in the development of light machine guns.

E: Württembergisches Gebirgs-Bataillon, Caporetto, October 1917

On a snow-covered Alpine peak, a rifleman from the Württemberg mountain rifle battalion looks ahead to the next Italian position. His commander, *Oberleutnant* (First lieutenant) Erwin Rommel – the future commander of Hitler's *Afrika Korps* – won Germany's highest decoration for valour during this battle. He led two companies through the Italian frontline, overrunning an artillery position, destroying an Italian counter-attack and capturing a regiment of *Besaglieri*. When the rest of his battalion caught up, Rommel led the way again, climbing Monte Matajur from the rear and compelling more Italians to surrender. The Württemberger battalion took 150 Italian officers and 9,000 other ranks prisoner, and captured 81 guns. Rommel was promoted to Captain and awarded the *Pour le Mérite*.

The mountain rifle battalion was created in 1915 and first fought in the Carpathian mountains against the Russians. The small-unit tactics demanded by mountain warfare were very similar to those of the

German stormtroops wearing gas masks in action at Ploegsteert Wood. The Germans were driven from this position, 10 km south of Ypres, in mid-1917, but although the British fortified it that winter, it was retaken by the Germans in April 1918. (IWM)

A Mark IV tank from 'C' battalion, RTR, captured by the Germans at Cambrai. Although the Germans assembled a large number of Allied tanks and cannibalised them for parts, only a *handful were ready for action in 1918. German repair shops lacked the correct tools and spares, and the vehicles were highly unreliable to start with. (US National Archives)*

stormtroopers, and they wore a uniform that anticipated the highly practical German uniform of World War II. With ankle boots and puttees, leather-patched trousers and Mauser carbines, they were the model for the 'stormtrooper look' that soon distinguished the divisional *Sturmabteilung* from the regular battalions. Note the field grey cap, which carries the Württemberg national cockade on the left and the national cockade on the right.

F: Guard Pioneer flamethrower team, Fort Douamont, May 1916

After its capture by the Germans, the concrete and steel fortress of Fort Douamont was pounded by French heavy artillery. Four giant 370 mm mortars pounded the fort around the clock. By night, up to 1,000 German infantrymen crowded inside to shelter from the bombardment. Here it is late afternoon, and a party of Guard Pioneers rest, with their combat equipment nearby. Behind them, a long column of men begins to filter into the fort, passing along the corridor and descending to the lower level. The bombardment fills the tunnels with fumes and the ventilation system has broken down. Both sides are employing poison gas so the soldiers keep their respirators handy. The men drink bottled mineral water, brought up by ration parties during the night and stored at the fort. They take extra precautions with their flamethrowers, after the disaster of 8 May, when Bavarian troops accidentally detonated a store of grenades by brewing coffee next to them. (The explosion ruptured tanks of flamethrower fuel which sent a fireball down to a magazine full of 155 mm shells. Over 650 men were killed, entombed in a section of the Fort that remains sealed off to this day.)

G: Helmets and insignia

1. 1916 pattern *Stahlhelm*. Note the lugs for attaching extra armour to the front
2. 1917 pattern *Stahlhelm* in typical camouflage pattern
3. 1918 pattern *Stahlhelm*

Sometimes described as 'for those using earphones' or as a cavalry helmet, this helmet was probably intended for all soldiers. The brim cutouts were supposed to lessen blast damage to the ears. The war ended before it could be widely distributed.

4. Shoulder straps:
- (a) Grenadier, 1st *Sturmbataillon*
- (b) Grenadier, 1st *Sturmbataillon*, 1918 variation
- (c) *Sturmbataillon Rohr*
- (d) Grenadier, *sturm-Kompanie*, 6th Bavarian *Sturmbataillon*
- (e) *Pionier, Minenwerfer Kompanie*
- (f) *Kanonier, Infanterie-Geschütz-batterien*
- (g) *Jäger*, 3rd *Jäger-Sturmbataillon* (with feldmütze)
- (h) *Artillerie Abteillung, Sturmbataillon Rohr.*

5. Grenadier NCO, 6th *Sturmbataillon*

The Bavarian army retained several distinctions, including the light blue diamond pattern woven over pale grey lace (silver for officers). Note that the *feldmütze* has the Bavarian national cockade. Troops occupying the frontline trenches normally wore the *feldmütze*, donning the helmet only when under bombardment or expecting action. Unfortunately, as Ernst Junger recalled, British snipers were particularly adept at putting a round through the head of anyone moving carelessly in a trench with a low parapet. The distinctive red cap band was too highly visible and special covers were soon issued. In July 1917 a new pattern *feldmütze* appeared, with a drab band for all arms and all ranks.

6. *Pionier*, 3rd Guard Reserve Pioneer Regiment

In 1915 an all-volunteer Pioneer detachment was created to operate the newly developed flame-

A 7.6 cm light Minenwerfer is dragged along by its crew. Note the gunners still have jackboots and Gewehr 98s. *With a maximum range of about 1,100 m, the light mortar could fire high explosive or gas shells. (IWM)*

Victory over Russia freed some 400,000 German troops for the 1918 offensive in France. But they needed retraining first: their equipment and tactics were out of date by the standards of the Western Front. (Private collection)

throwers. It was expanded into the 3rd Guard Reserve Pioneer Regiment, which included no less than 12 companies by 1917. Note the 'deathshead' badge worn on the left cuff and the Guard *lutzen* on the collar.

7. Stormtrooper, 23rd Stormtroop Company, 1st Saxon Reserve Division

In a typical combination of pre-war uniform and late war equipment, this stormtrooper wears the Saxon 1910 pattern field service dress, which retained the distinctive Saxon piping, cuffs and skirt-flaps. But the stormtrooper has added leather elbow patches, an armband and 1917 pattern trousers made of cloth eeked out with nettle fibres.

8. NCOs from *Sturmbataillon Nr. 1* (from a photograph)

The soldier on the left is a marksman, and wears the German army musketry badge, the *Schützenschnur*: a plaited cord from the right shoulder to the top button of the tunic plus badge on left collar. Machine gun marksmen had an oval badge with a machine gun symbol worn on the left sleeve. The soldier in the centre has an armband and dark breeches.

9. Grenadier, unidentified stormtroop battalion

This stormtrooper has the typical sandbag full of

German dead, possibly caught by artillery while trying to dig in. By concentrating their best troops in the 'attack' divisions of 1918, the Germans created some *excellent shock units – but these suffered the majority of the 900,000 casualties sustained during Ludendorff's offensives. (Private collection)*

stick grenades secured across his chest. Note the grenade badge on his left sleeve. Divisional storm-troop companies and battalions could be a law unto themselves regarding uniform, frequently adding locally made insignia.

H: Stormtrooper equipment

1–3. Assault Packs

German infantry were supposed to carry a spare pair of trousers, their *feldmütze*, two shirts, a spare pair of socks, two handkerchiefs, a rice bag, a house-wife, change of underwear, pair of shoes, boot brushes, salt and iron rations in their cowhide back pack. This was too bulky for the stormtroopers and from 1915 an 'assault pack' was increasingly fa-voured. In these three variations, taken from an officer's trench sketch book, soldiers have taken the blackened M1910 aluminium canteen and wrapped their greatcoat inside the M1892 tent cloth. In (3) the

soldier has attached empty sandbags to carry extra kit or to consolidate captured enemy positions.

4. The M1910 canteen had a detachable cup/frying pan with handle as its lid. It held 4¼ pints. It was supposed to be aluminium painted black, but from 1915 cheaper enamelled metal versions were issued, often painted field grey.

5. 1917 pattern *Stielhandgranate* with carrying bags made from sandbags, designed to be worn across the chest. Ernst Junger led a trench raid with four stick grenades in either bag and another five 'egg' grenades in his tunic pockets.

6. Cartridge pouches

Each pouch held three five-round strips, for a total of 45 rounds in each triple pouch. Two triple pouches gave 90 rounds on the belt plus (according to regulations) another 90 in the back pack. The leather pouches were originally brown in 1914 but in Sep-tember 1915 all leather equipment was ordered to be blackened at the behest of the General Staff.

7. *Jäger* bayonet with green *troddel* (bayonet knot)

8. Wirecutters

9. Bayonet of wartime manufacture, with steel hilt, painted grey. The scabbard is the M1898 steel reinforced leather with *toddel*. The latter varied according to rank and company.

10. The M1887 entrenching tool was looped on to the left of the belt and the strap also secured the bayonet scabbard to the spade handle. From 1915 soldiers began to use sharpened shovels in close, quarter fighting. For digging in, longer-handled shovels were more efficient and stormtroops went into action in 1918 with the M1822 shovel attached to their belts in a variety of improvised fittings.

11. Triple cartridge pouches

12. M1907 Waterbottle. Made of cloth-covered aluminium, this had a capacity of 1¾ pints. Numerous other types were used during the war.

13. M1887 haversack, popularly known as the 'bread bag'. Made of pale brown cloth, it was attached to the belt by two buttoned loops and the metal hook in the middle. The rings on the inner face enable a sling to be fitted so that it could be worn around the body. It was used to carry an aluminium drinking cup, knife and fork and other personal kit.

14. Gas mask filter-carrying case

15. Carrying cases for the M1915 respirator. The brown cloth bag was looped to the belt and worn underneath the left triple cartridge pouch. A more robust metal container was introduced at the beginning of 1916.

Unlike Sir Douglas Haig, the German C-in-C did not even see a tank until February 1918, let alone press for their mass production. Only four A7Vs like this went into action on 21 March 1918. One former stormtrooper who transferred to the new tank units was Sergeant Sepp Dietrich – later an SS tank general. (IWM)

I: 3rd Jäger-Sturmbataillon counter-attacks at Cambrai

The 3rd *Jäger* assault battalion was one of the few stormtroop battalions available for the counter-attack at Cambrai. Most *Jäger*, mountain rifle and storm-troop battalions were still in Italy where they had led the attack at Caporetto. Here a *Jäger* company recaptures part of the original German frontline. Squads of riflemen advance, covered by fire from their machine gun platoons. A light (7.6 cm) *minenwerfer* is brought forward, pulled along by leather straps. By bringing their heavy weapons forward with the leading troops, the Germans were able to overwhelm British strongpoints without the time-consuming business of organising an artillery bombardment. Without radios, it was hard to coordinate an infantry advance with the supporting artillery, and the rolling barrage invariably moved too quickly or too slowly. Although not designated as assault battalions, many *Jäger* battalions were almost indistinguishable from the stormtroops by 1917. The first German infantry units to receive machine guns, they began the war with a machine gun platoon per battalion, rather than one per regiment. Their tradition of light infantry tactics lent itself to the new methods developed from 1915, and they joined the *Stosstruppen* in the first wave during the Kaiser's Battle. The *Jäger* battalions of the German Army included several junior officers destined for fame, if not glory, in World War II Rommel joined the Württemberg mountain rifles in 1915; his successor in Tunisia, Dieter von Arnim finished World War I as ordnance officer for the 4th *Jäger* division; Heinz Guderian began the war in the 10th *Jäger* battalion, and was at the first battle of Ypres in 1914 as assistant signals officer of the 4th Army; and Friedrich Paulus was the regimental staff officer of the 2nd (Prussian) *Jäger* battalion which, as part of the Alpine Corps, took part in the battle of Verdun. His name is indelibly linked to a later holocaust: he commanded the ill-fated 6th Army at Stalingrad.

The name 'stormtrooper' was still synonymous with victory, even after the German defeat. It was soon revived by the fledgling Nazi party: the SA (Sturmabteilung) was a paramilitary organisation formed to strongarm other parties, especially the communists (Private collection)

J: NCO, Angriffsdivision, March 1918

The Kaiser's Battle begins: a stormtrooper waits in a frontline trench, ready to go 'over the top' the moment the barrage lifts to the British second line. He is fresh and ready for battle, having been kept behind the lines until the night before. The front was held by second line units, destined to play no part in the offensive – so if British trench raiders captured anyone, they would learn no significant details. The stormtrooper wears the 1915 *Bluse*, the *Stahlhelm*, puttees and ankle boots. When he attacks, he will rely more on his stick grenades than his Mauser carbine slung over his back. Whereas at Verdun (and in later attacks with limited objectives) the stormtroops had attacked enemy strongpoints and then waited to be relieved by line infantry battalions, now they were to press ahead regardless. As at Cambrai and Caporetto, they were to advance as rapidly and as far as possible, breaking into open country and completely dislocating the British defences. But stormtroop battalions relied on their heavy weapons – mortars, machine guns and light field guns – and these all had to be moved by hand. Despite their best efforts, the heavy weapons companies would struggle to keep up, blunting the offensive power of the battalions.

K: Stormtroops capture a British battery, March 1918

A group of stormtroops stand among the abandoned 18-pdr. field guns of a British artillery battery. Spent shell cases litter the ground, a testimony to the gunners' resistance, but the guns could not be evacuated by the horse teams once under machine gun fire. The victorious stormtroops have been in constant action for 48 hours, and the strain is beginning to show. Some soldiers prepare to resume the advance, led by an NCO with an MP18 9 mm sub-machine gun, but others have had enough and are looting the British stores. The High Command's propaganda about the success of the U-Boats is exposed as a lie: the British supply dumps contain all manner of items no longer seen in Germany. Behind the stormtroops an infantry gun team haul along their cut-down Russian 7.62 cm *Infanterie-Geschütz*. Although they had won an impressive victory, the stormtroops' pursuit was conducted at walking pace, while the Allies redeployed by railway; the German infantry had developed battle-winning tactics, but lacked the mobility to convert tactical triumph into strategic success.

L: Coming Home! Freikorps unit in action, small German town 1919

Parts of some Army units passed directly into the Freikorps organisation – the powerful East Prussian Freikorps (*Ostpreussiches*) included detachments from Ulanen regiment No. 8, *Jäger zu Pferde* No. 10 and *Husaren* regiment No. 8 for example.

The Freikorps attracted many elite troops who felt that they had been 'stabbed in the back', and were thus opposed to the political far left which had betrayed the Fatherland. Many regular units were formed from disbanded troops to support detachments of loyal regulars.

As seen with these three soldiers engaged in fierce street fighting against what they deem to be left-wing traitors, their uniforms are predominantly fashioned in the Stormtrooper mould. There are examples that in some cases units also retained their regimental insignia, and wore unofficial badges such as skull and cross bones, and wolf's head.

References

The Official History of Operations in France and Belgium 1917. Vol. II gives the credit to Captain André Laffargue. His pamphlet 'The attack in Trench Warfare' was commercially published in 1916, and some copies were circulated among German units.

Oberste Heeresleitung: the supreme command of the field army. Ultimate authority was vested in the Kaiser, while the Chief of the General Staff exercised practical control.

Attacks, Athena Press, 1989.

The 75th to 82nd reserve divisions plus the 8th Bavarian reserve division.

The 231st to 242nd divisions plus the 15th Bavarian.

Angriffsdivisionen – but sometimes referred to as *Stossdivisionen* or *Mobilmachungsdivisionen*.

War. English edition, Martin Secker Ltd., London 1929 p.298.

See Martin Samuels, *Doctrine and Dogma* (Greenwood Press, 1992) and Martin Middlebrook, *The Kaiser's Battle* (Allan Lane, 1978).

For instance, in August to September 1914 the 35th Fusiliers marched 408 miles in 27 consecutive days, fighting 11 battles in the process.

Ernst Jünger, *Storm of Steel* (London, 1929).

[11]Bruce I. Gudmundsson, *Stormtroop Tactics* (Praeger 1989) p.89.

[12]Richard Baumgartner (Ed), *The Passage*, Griffin Books, 1984.

[13]Gustav Ebelhauser (Edited by Richard Baugartner), *The Passage – A Tragedy of the First World War*, Griffon Books, 1984.

[14]Ammunition expenditure varied widely, but at the height of the battle, British artillery was delivering up to 500 tons of explosive per day on the frontage of a single division (approximately 2,000 yards).

[15]Ludwig Renn, *War*, London, 1929.

[16]General von Kuhl, Chief of Staff to Crown Prince Rupprecht, quoted in *Military Operations in France and Belgium, 1917.*

[17]*Military Operations in France and Belgium*, 1917.

[18]General Sir Edward Spears, *Liason 1914*, London, 1968.

[19]*Infantry in Battle*, Washington DC, 1939.

[20]Ernst Junger, *Storm of Steel* (London, 1929), p.242

INDEX

(References to illustrations are shown in **bold**. Plates are shown with caption locators in brackets)